THE IMPORT BOOK
REVISED

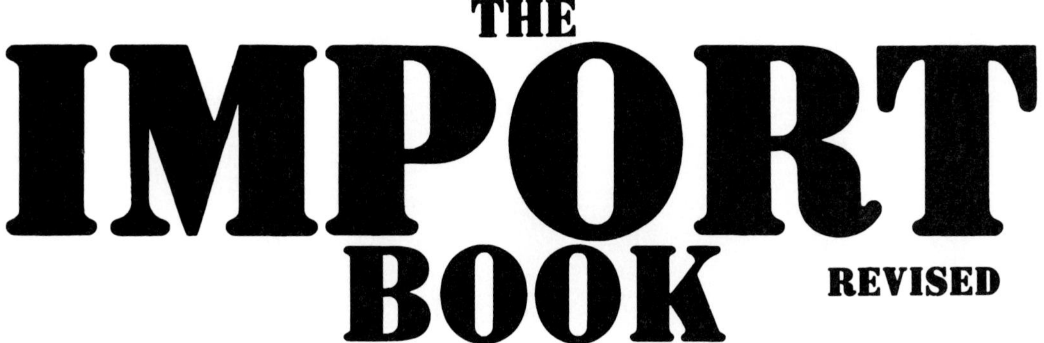

THE IMPORT BOOK
REVISED

How to select, locate and import your own European car

Larry Smith

Motorbooks International
Publishers & Wholesalers Inc
Osceola, Wisconsin 54020, USA

First published in 1986 by Motorbooks International Publishers & Wholesalers Inc, PO Box 2, 729 Prospect Avenue, Osceola, WI 54020 USA

Based on *The Import Book* originally published by Larry Smith Associates, Inc., in 1984.

Motorbooks International is a certified trademark, registered with the United States Patent Office

Printed and bound in the United States of America

The information in this book is true and complete to the best of our knowledge. All recommendations are made without any guarantee on the part of the author or publisher, who also disclaim any liability incurred in connection with the use of this data or specific details

Library of Congress Cataloging-in-Publication Data

Smith, Larry.
  The import book revised.
    1. Automobile industry and trade—Europe.
2. Automobiles, Foreign—United States—Purchasing.
I. Title.
HD9710.E82S66 1986   382'.456292'029   86-18004
ISBN 0-87938-231-7 (soft)

Cover photo: 1986 Porsche Carrera cabriolet, by Gordon Maltby

Contents

Acknowledgments

Grateful acknowledgment is made to the following people for their support and assistance: Louise Mirrasoul; Marilyn Keto; Thompson Day Graphics; Thompson Smith; Anne Smith; James T. Welte, Senior Import Specialist, U.S. Customs, San Francisco; William R. McCreight, West Germany.

Introduction

This book is designed not only to assist the reader in threading his or her way through US Customs regulations, Department of Transportation (DOT) and Environmental Protection Agency (EPA) requirements but also to make importing a car a more enjoyable experience. This book is *not* designed for the professional who imports many cars, but for the individual who imports a single car. The process throughout the book is illustrated by the author's experience in importing a car, a Porsche, from West Germany.

There is a way to buy a European car and save substantial sums while avoiding excessive US markups and overhead costs on imported cars such as BMW, Mercedes-Benz, Porsche, Ferrari, Renault, Jaguar and Audi. In addition, you can obtain that limited-production car or collector item worth perhaps several times what you would pay for it in the country of origin. Many of the most popular cars in Europe are not even imported into the United States. For instance, Mercedes offers only eleven models for the United States while offering seventeen in Europe. And with component combinations, this number is probably nearer thirty models.

Prices and taxes

Price differences

Cars in Europe can be priced as much as thirty to fifty percent less than a comparable car in the United States. The comparison below between West Germany and United States new car prices shows some of the savings that can be made when purchasing a new car in Europe.

Make and model	West Germany*	US
Mercedes-Benz 560SL	na	$54,860
Mercedes-Benz 190E	$14,010	29,120
Mercedes-Benz 300TD	20,766	41,600
BMW 325	12,941	21,500
BMW 635CSi	24,860	46,000
Audi 4000	7,607	14,230
Porsche 944	18,384	24,500
Porsche Carrera	27,250	38,750
Porsche 928S	41,458	51,900

*Exchange rate as of March 1986 ($1=2.55 DM)
Sources: *Motor Auto und Sport* (West Germany), US dealers
na: Price not available

Most people are unaware of these large differences. Many differences can be traced to the strong US dollar, the lack of a number of accessories the West Germans, and most Europeans, consider nonessential, such as air conditioning and leather interior, and non-conformance to US environmental and safety laws. Some of the differences certainly are justified, but prospective purchasers can usually save a bundle by purchasing a car in Europe and importing it themselves.

Another consideration for the differences in prices is that while the price in Europe may be substantially less than that of an equivalent car in the United States the differences can widen when the car in question has been a regular production model but has not been imported to the United States, or is a limited production model. An excellent example of this is the Porsche 911 Carrera 3.0 produced only in 1976 and 1977 in very limited quantity (less than 3,000 worldwide). This car is relatively rare in the United States, which increases its value. This car can be purchased in West Germany at between $8,000 and $10,000, and is conservatively worth $25,000 to $32,000 in the United States.

Examples of prices of used models from West Germany are shown below.

Make and model	West Germany*	US
1973 Mercedes-Benz 350SL	$ 5,871	$21,000
1975 Mercedes-Benz 450SL	9,091	19,900
1985 Mercedes-Benz 500SEC	27,645	45,000

Make and model	West Germany*	US
1980 BMW 323i	4,219	na
1981 BMW 635CSi	8,167	na*
1983 BMW 635CSi	21,667	na
1974 911 Porsche Carrera	2,083	17,500
1976 911 Porsche Carrera	9,000	26,500
1977 911 Porsche Carrera	9,062	28,000
1980 911SC Porsche	9,969	23,000
1980 911SC Porsche	10,409	23,000
1985 911 Porsche Carrera	24,531	42,000

*Prices for new and used cars shown are plus DOT/ EPA, taxes, shipping, etc.

Exchange rate as of March 1986 ($1=2.55 DM)

Sources: *Porsche Panorama, San Francisco Chronicle*

na: Not available (Since 1985 the BMW 635 has become available in the United States)

Typical costs involved in importing a car that you should consider are: price of car, shipping, US Customs duty, DOT/EPA conformation. Example: The total cost for a 1976 911 Porsche Carrera 3.0 including all the above items was $15,066 for a car appraised in the United States from $25,000 to $37,000.

At the present time, purchasing a new car of one of the major manufacturers is difficult to do because the manufacturer could take away the franchise of the dealer in Europe selling to Americans for export out of that country to the United States. (Therefore it is recommended that you contact independent sources to purchase a new car.)

Some factories (Mercedes most notably) will not allow an agent to purchase a car and deliver it to the owner; the car must be picked up by the owner. Others appear to have less stringent rules in this respect. Check with the factory directly before entering an order. However, be prepared for a kindly reference to your US dealer, as the factory will usually not take an order unless it's through a dealer. Be sure to contact a dealer of the model car you desire in the country of origin to check on availability of the particular model. Many new models have a long waiting period; often a year or more.

If you are willing to settle for a used car rather than a new car, you can find some excellent values. And there are more to choose from. However, the good ones usually don't stay on the market long. This book focuses on acquiring a used car, as I did.

There are brokers who have purchased contracts for delivery positions; but be careful, as in most cases you will be paying a premium over the dealer price. These brokers, however, in most cases can deliver almost immediately.

Mercedes-Benz as well as most of the other auto manufacturers has its own export and import compa-nies, and will not sell models outside these channels. The business of buying contracts for delivery of new Mercedes in West Germany is often brisk, and one sees ads in the newspapers for new cars usually at a premium over the new price.

Value Added Tax (VAT)

The principle of the Value Added Tax works like this: If someone cuts down a tree and sells it to me for $100, he must charge a fourteen percent VAT ($14). If I saw it into lumber and resell it for $200 I must add a VAT of $28 to my sales price, but I get a credit for the $14 VAT I already paid (the VAT I charge is for the value I add). If you buy the lumber from me and make a table that you sell for $400 you have to charge fourteen percent VAT ($56), but you get a credit of $28 for the VAT you paid. In the end the consumer pays a fourteen percent VAT on the end sales price and all other VAT along the way has been refunded, except the value added in each link. It is an administrative nightmare and there is really no practicality in it, but it is used all over Europe.

There is no VAT on exports, because it would make European industry noncompetitive. This means, in practice, VAT must be paid and is then refunded from the seller when the buyer can prove with a special form and customs stamps that the article has in fact left the country.

To the individual, the big advantage in price over these export companies is in buying local models. Mercedes gives no discounts, but a four percent discount can often be obtained from other companies on a cash sale with no trade-in on new cars.

For used cars, it is usually better to buy directly from the owner rather than from a dealer or a broker (who will add mark-up). One exception is that many new-car dealers take old cars in trade, but do not legally buy them. They put them on their lot and sell them as an agent of the owner, sometimes for less than the trade-in value. The difference is, in effect, a discount. This is usually the discount given on a cash sale with no trade-in. This system avoids some German legal and tax problems for the dealer and results in a lower price for you.

Remember that the VAT is paid on new cars but is not applicable to the buyer of private property—a used car is private property. VAT has already been paid on the article by the original consumer. The tax applies to companies in business to manufacture or resell the goods.

While it may appear initially financially feasible to purchase and import a car into the United States, the complications imposed by US, local or state regulatory agencies may make the process difficult or impossible.

Vehicles purchased outside the United States, even though the same or similar models are regularly imported, may not conform to US emissions and safety requirements. The procedures to bring such cars into conformance are most important, and make it possible to have the car you desire. And you can do as I did—handle the conformation work yourself.

There have been many articles about the so-called gray market and the problems inherent in purchasing a car and bringing it into the United States. Much information has been unclear and most of what you hear is third hand (or more distant) and not reliable. This book attempts to set the record straight concerning this area of auto importing.

Summary

In conclusion, you should be optimistic in the possibility of importing your own car from Europe. Follow the steps in this book carefully and you should come out on top. But beware; there are always some disadvantages.

US-sourced recalls may not apply to your vehicle and this may mean your car will miss out on some modifications which may be desirable.

Non-US-specification parts may be hard to find in the United States when your car requires repair or maintenance. Just be aware of all the possibilities.

Chapter 1

Locating your car

There are basically two ways to obtain your car: get help or do it yourself. They both work; you just have to decide which method is best for you.

Dealer

Although it is most likely that factory-authorized dealers will not be able to help you obtain a car directly, they may know of other ways in which you could get a car. Some of these dealers are not at the mercy of factory procedures, such as those in Belgium, Switzerland, France and Denmark. Because of the lower number of sales they experience, it is to their advantage to sell as many cars as possible, and restrictions could be relaxed. You only need to inquire as to the possibility.

Most US import car dealers have European delivery programs where the buyer purchases a car and the dealer arranges for the purchaser to pick the car up either from the factory or through a European dealer. When the purchaser arrives overseas he picks up the car and then can drive it, delivering the car to a location for shipment to the United States. Shipment is usually made by boat, which can take anywhere from forty-five to seventy-five days. The price for the car usually covers everything, including a small discount because the dealer doesn't have to pre-deliver the car. This alternative is usually for a new car; though sometimes a dealer will import a used car. A dealer, however, will not usually sell or handle a car not already conforming to US EPA and safety requirements; thus, cars not conforming are usually not imported by a dealer.

Many independent dealers have new models available and can obtain excellent used cars with low mileages, either on consignment or as trade-ins. Some of these dealers are able to procure cars through other sources and are not at the mercy of the factory licenses.

Private company

You might consider using the services of an experienced group or individual, who, for a fee, will locate, select and arrange transportation for US citizens (and others) exporting cars. Many provide a service in not only locating a specific car, but also arranging transportation and insurance, acting as your agent in purchasing the car, taking care of the paperwork, assisting in bringing the car into the United States, and a multitude of other things. If you decide to use people like these, check them out very carefully. Here are a few suggestions:

1. Obtain and verify references from people they have assisted before
2. Make sure they have a good working knowledge of the foreign licensing, insurance laws and regulations

3. Request that they provide on-the-spot representation (which is better than having to go over themselves each time to look for a car)
4. Fluency in the native language is important, thus enabling them to bargain to obtain the best prices
5. They must have an intimate and thorough knowledge of the characteristics of autos in the market, which should enable them to select only superior cars
6. A working knowledge of US Customs procedures and paperwork is essential
7. They must have knowledge of US DOT and EPA requirements

If you do not understand the language it is better to have someone assist in this regard and even handle the negotiations between you and the seller as if they were buying the car themselves, acting as your agent.

Individual

Having friends in Europe is a good avenue to explore for locating a car, if they know what to look for; that is, key points and possible problem areas of the specific car. In addition, be sure they would have the time and effort to actively look for the car. The purchase most likely would be from a private party, which is going to take coordination to first find the car and then the agreement to purchase it, transfer of the money from the United States, considerations for insurance and shipping, inspecting the car to make sure it is sound mechanically and free from rust and damage are only some of the factors. If your friends have never done anything like this before it may be an imposition upon them because it takes time, expertise and expense.

The ideal is, of course, for you to take a trip. That way you can have the fun of locating, selecting, testing and purchasing your own car. If you are fluent in the language of the country and dress and act like a native who has lived there all his or her life, then it should be easy for you to handle the entire process yourself.

If you don't speak the language fluently and don't have a native friend to assist, you may pay a premium just because you are a foreigner. However, in spite of any premium, the cost of the car may still be considerably less than what you would pay for the same car in the United States. If you have done your homework you will know very closely your costs in all regards.

Advertisement

If you desire to import a new car versus a used car, then you will have to do a little research consisting of determining how to get in touch with the factory without going through the dealer. There are a number of individuals and companies that handle new cars (and used) such that you will not need to go through the US dealer. Several are advertised regularly in US auto journals and other publications. Most offer both cars meeting US EPA and safety requirements, and cars not meeting these requirements. In the latter case, you will have to handle EPA and safety requirements yourself. These companies are the importers themselves, and probably pass on the costs for importation (plus some) to the purchaser.

Locating your own car requires that you perform substantial research to find the auto you want, which means reading import auto sports journals, magazines and local newspapers from Europe to keep track of offerings for used and new cars. Of course, you need to be fluent in the native language in order to read these publications, and if you have these publications sent to you from Europe they will take anywhere from seven to ten days (or more) to reach you. Usually by then the cars will have been sold. Another approach is to find a newsstand in your home town that has the publications you need. In this way, you can be kept up to date earlier than if you receive a paper from Europe directly through the mails. (One of the best newspapers in Frankfurt, West Germany, is the *Frankfurter RundSchau*. The Saturday edition usually has the best ads for cars.)

Locating your own car can also be very frustrating and expensive if not properly organized. You could actually travel throughout the country purchasing the local newspapers or visiting local auto dealers and private parties. Most sales from dealers will be higher in price than if the car is purchased from a private party, and for this reason private parties are preferred. Prices also have been known to rise rapidly when the sellers know they are selling to a foreigner rather than to a native.

Round-trip airfare can easily cost $1,500 plus the added costs of transportation within the country. For a week to two weeks, costs could approach $3,000 or more. In addition, there are many European laws and regulations that must be followed as to purchase and exportation of a car to ensure the car will be allowed to leave the country. Laws differ within each area of the country also.

Advertisements in newspapers and magazines and personal contacts can bring leads for cars. Advertisements in local newspapers in West Germany are not like they are in the United States. First, they appear only on Wednesdays, Fridays and Saturdays, and not in all papers. And there are locations where newsstands carry newspapers from all over the country. Thus, you could go to a major city like Frankfurt and, buying the right newspapers, you could get a good line on most cars for sale throughout West Germany.

In addition, appearing every Saturday in West Germany is an excellent magazine, *Auto Motor und Sport*. It has a section devoted to advertisements of autos for sale by individuals, dealers and wrecking yards. For example, an ad might appear like this: "323i Autom., Servo, 7.83, 45000 km, weiss, SSD, Extr., unf.frei." And you can translate that into "BMW 323i with automatic transmission and power steering, first purchased in July 1983. It now was 27,900 miles, is white with sun roof and extras. Free of damage."

As you can see from this one example, abbreviations are often used in ads. Here is a list of some of the more common German ones:

AHK	Trailer hitch
ATG	With exchange transmission
ATM	With exchange motor
BJ	Model year (same as month/yr. mfg)
EZ	First time registered (bought new)
FP	Firm price
ESD	Electric sliding roof
LM	Alloy wheels and "goodies"
NP	New price (or price when new)
RC	Radio with cassette recorder
VB	Asking price
VS	Offering price
VP	Selling price

If you're not fluent in German, the following list of terms will help you decipher an ad.

English	**German**
Accessories	Zubehor
Appearance	Aufmachung
Air Conditioning	Klimaanlage
Agent	Agentur
Asking	VB (Verhandlungsbasis)
All models	Alle modelle
Alloy wheels	LM-felgen
All extras	Alle Extras
Best condition	Bestzustand
Brown metallic	Braun-met
Bumpers	Stosstange
Blue metallic	Blaumettalic
Change	Umbau
Completely equipped	Komplett ausgestattet
Central locking system	Zentralverriegelung
Decorative wheels	Schmiedefelgen
Electric heated windows	Beheizbar
Electric sunroof	Schiebedach (elcktrisch)
Electric windows	Elektr Fensterheber
Electric mirrors	Spiegel (elektrisch)
Fur-skinned seats	Fellsitzbezuege
For sale	rum Verkauf
Front & back	vorne + hinten
First owner	Erstbesitzer

English	**German**
Garaged	Garagenwagen
Fiberglass sunroof	Glasdach
Fender-skirts	Kotflugel
Fog lamps	Nebellampen
Headrests	Kopfstutzen
Including tax	inkl. MwSt
Leather upholstery	Lederpolster
"Looking for"	Suche
Looks new	neuwertig
Many extras	Weitere Extras
Month/Yr. manufactured	4/84
Never wrecked	Unfallfrei
Offer	Angebot
Power steering	Servo (lenkung)
Plus tax	+ MwSt
Possible to trade	Eintausch moeglich
Preferred	bevorzugt
Radio-cassette	Radio CR
Rear wipers	Heckwischer
Steel sunroof	SSD
Sale by private party	Verkauft privat.
Sunroof	Schiebedach
Super well cared for	super gepflegt
Silver	Silber
Tinted windows	colorverglasung
Velour upholstery	Velours
Technical inspection due	TUV (and date)
Wrecked	Unfall

Telephone numbers are included in most ads. If you know the area codes, a glance at the number will give you a clue to the geographic area in which the car is located. You can then determine which car to go see.

German inspection

My company, Larry Smith Associates, Inc., has assisted several people to import cars into the United States from West Germany. So it is the country of West Germany that I am most familiar with, in terms of importing. Each country is a little different, and you need to know as much as possible about its rules, regulations and customs.

For example, every two years every car in Germany has to pass a very tough technical inspection that covers every aspect of safety and smog control. It is very hard to pass the first time, even for a two-year-old car. Most people have their own dealer inspect the car first and repair anything he finds and still many have to go back again for retesting. For example, a friend's Mercedes failed because the brake lines were dirty and it could not be seen if they were pitted or not, and the stress-bearing portions of the frame had rust on them.

It is not legal to drive a car in Germany, or to even register it, without unlimited liability insurance, which is very expensive. The insurance companies are required by law to notify the police if insurance lapses—they may come the same day and confiscate the plates. A car can be registered for export and with a special plate if proof of short-term, paid-up insurance is provided.

There are no export permits on cars. All you need do is deliver it to an airline or forwarding agent and pay the fees for shipping, or simply drive it out of the country. But in order to drive it you must have the special plate as described above.

Germany has its own equivalent of the DOT and EPA standards and in some cases they are tougher than those in the United States. An export model cannot be registered in West Germany unless it is changed back to German standards. For example, the left and right sides must be wired separately and fused so that all electrical functions cannot fail at the same time. Also, US lights cannot pass German standards.

The best way to sum up the German inspection program is this: A BMW 635CSi will go 150 mph and there are no speed limits on Autobahns. Everything about a car, including quality of tires must be able to withstand sustained top-speed operation all day, day after day, because there are people who drive this way. For example, there is a list of tires you are allowed to use on a Porsche—nothing else is accepted. The inspection program is run by the Association of Engineers and is designed to prevent accidents due to mechanical, electrical or tire failure.

Determining year of manufacture

On the German registration card it tells the month and year the car was manufactured and when first registered. It does not say what year's model it is. In effect the manufacturers need several months from time of manufacture to get the car through the dealer network and to the buyer. This means that they begin shipping the next year's model a few months before year end. This differs slightly by manufacturer. US manufacturers do the same. If this were not the case, cars delivered in the first four months of 1985, for instance, would have to be designated 1984 models.

Chapter 2

Selecting your car

Selecting a car may take many phone calls and visits as soon as an ad appears, because depending upon the type of car, age, accessories and price it could be sold or taken off the market quickly. After telephone contact is made, and the car appears to meet your requirements, an appointment should be made to personally inspect it.

The car should first be inspected very carefully to ascertain that it is complete and has no major body or frame damage. The entire car should be inspected for rust. If it passes this inspection, the car then should be driven to determine its condition and soundness. The car should also be put up on a rack or hoist to facilitate inspection. Worn tires, shocks, rust, pitted metal and so on reduce the price of the car, and enable you to bargain more easily.

In West Germany each car must pass a stiff inspection to be licensed. If it doesn't pass this inspection it can't be licensed or insured, and can't be driven. Thus, a car that has not passed its inspection will be of less value than another that has passed. Knowledge of this fact alone can enable you to bargain more effectively with the seller.

The process of selection of a car should be done much as you would for a used car in the United States, but with much more care and a more critical eye, because once the car has been purchased and exported it is very costly to return it to be fixed or to get your money back. Repair costs must be considered and added to the overall price of the car, and compared with its value after importation.

The following gives a general idea of the areas that should be inspected:

History

Obtain as much history of the car as possible, such as previous owner(s), maintenance records, was it garaged or not, where was it driven, past and present problems. All these facts can assist in your evaluation of the car.

Body

Check for dings and rust. Look closely for rust at points where metal is joined. Check inside fenders and where rubber moldings cover metal. Has the car been repainted? Depending upon age of car this could be a problem. Repaint may signify a concerned owner who wishes to preserve his car, but could mask damage by accident or rust.

Rust may only be surface related, but may require extensive repair or replacement of parts. Check for rust under the car, on the body pan, on points where torsion bars join the front body, heater exits, and under side panels under doors. If these parts show rust, major problems could develop. (In the manufacturing process since 1976, Porsche zinc coated the body and gave a warranty for seven years against rust.) Minor dings or scratches can easily be repaired, even surface rust can be removed, but other deeper rust could indicate a problem car.

Interior

Interiors come in a variety of combinations including vinyl, cloth and leather; vinyl and cloth; or leather. For example, in Germany, most Porsches are fitted with a combination of vinyl and cloth. Seats usually have cloth inserts.

The interior should be free of ripped or stained materials. Costs to replace fabrics can be high. If the interior materials need replacing, either the car should be rejected, the price should be considerably reduced, of the seller should bring the interior up to standard, before it is sold.

Engine and transmission

The condition of the engine can only be determined by running it and listening for abnormal sounds, both standing idle and at speed. Check engine underneath for bent oil lines and leaking oil. Leaking oil lines can be replaced, but a leaking engine usually means breaking the case and replacing engine seals. For Porsches, this can be costly.

The characteristic noises emanating from a Porsche do not necessarily mean a worn engine.

If you are not capable of checking out the engine, take the car to a reputable mechanic, preferably one who deals in the model car in which you are interested and who himself has no interest in the car. For a small fee he will check the engine and transmission and even inspect the entire car if you desire.

The transmission should be checked for smooth shifting and no bearing noise. Difficulty in shifting up or down may mean worn synchros or clutch which could be expensive to replace.

Tires and wheels

Worn tires will, in most instances, need to be replaced. Worn tires can also indicate that the suspension may be out of alignment. Misalignment can be the result of damage from an accident. If so, major repairs may be needed. Such a car should be rejected.

Wheels, for the most part, can be cleaned by professionals. Bent, badly pitted or cracked wheels should be replaced. A car with these items should be reduced in price if the wheels are not replaced by the seller.

Sunroof

Check to see that mechanisms work smoothly and properly. Lack of lubrication could mean the owner has also neglected other areas of the car. Targa tops should be checked to see that the fabric fits all around, is tight on all edges, and has no leaks. Wind noise at high speed indicates a poor-fitting top that probably leaks. Leaking could also mean that the rubber around the windshield needs replacing which can be expensive. The Targa top is adjustable and easily replaceable, which could eliminate some problems. A new top costs about $1,800 in the United States. Refurbishing the old top using the original mechanism runs about $400.

Check list

The following list is used to judge cars for concourse condition (according to the Porsche Club of America, Golden Gate Region) and can be used as a guideline when inspecting your car. Any missing or damaged areas should be noted and taken into consideration in the final selection process.

A. Exterior
1. Coachwork (metalwork and fit)
2. Exterior paint
3. All exterior glass, including lights, mirrors, reflectors
4. Metal trim
5. Rubber trim (excluding bumpers)
6. Bumper assemblies
7. Hubcaps and outer surfaces of wheels and tires

B. Interior
1. Seats, mechanism of seats and belts
2. Upholstery of door panels, side paneling and headliner
3. Carpeting and floor covering, including the surface under floor mats
4. Interior of door compartments, pockets and glovebox
5. Dashboard, including street wheel instruments, and underside of dash down to floor
6. Doorjams, door hinges, rubber and fresh air vents on older models
7. Interior glass, lights and mirrors

C. Storage compartment
1. Trunk compartment, including paint and side covering
2. Underside of trunk lid, including latches, hinges and rubber molding
3. Floor covering
4. Windshield washer container and pump
5. Tools, jack, tire strag, spare tire and pump
6. Gas tank and filler separates
7. Battery

Warranties

Warranties on new cars purchased in Europe are generally by US dealers without concern. However, even though the factory will not say it will not cover warranty work or even service a car not purchased in Europe through your friendly US dealer, the dealers attempt all excuses not to provide service. Most say the additional work to bring the car up to US specs as required by EPA and DOT voids the warranty. This is utter nonsense.

But, there is a way to overcome this: purchase a warranty for either the new or the used car through International Warranty Corporation, 5030 Camino de la Siesta, Suite 106, San Diego, CA 92108 (800) 532-4800 or (800) 452-6700 (California).

Price negotiation

Millions of words have been written on how to buy and sell cars. What you do in Europe is much the same as what you've probably done in the United States. Remember: Once you have done it, there's no going back.

Chapter 3

Arranging for transportation

Once the car has been purchased and necessary paperwork completed to effect transfer of title, the next step involves the transport of the car to the United States, either by ship or air.

Transportation by ship can be by one of two methods. The first is by container where the auto is sealed in a container which is then loaded onto the ship. Heavier containers usually will be loaded down into the lower hold of the ship with lighter containers going on the top deck. This method is ok if the container goes into the hold where it is protected from the weather; not if it goes on top where it is not protected from weather. For example, one shipment via sealed container brought the container on top deck. Upon unloading, the car had to be jacked up and rolled out of the container because the front brakes were rusted locked and the front of the car somehow had salt spray blown over it so it had to be repainted. An expensive shipment, to say the least.

The second way to transport is by auto ship, that is, a specially designed ship where the auto is driven onto the ship and into the hold, then driven off the ship onto the dock in the United States.

Shipment by container is more costly than shipping by auto ship. Container costs are about $1,400 whereas shipment by auto ship would be about $850 (for a Porsche).

The other alternative, preferred by the author, is shipment by air. If shipment is by air, two possible ways exist: booked, meaning it gets scheduled into the regular shipment; or standby, meaning it will be scheduled into the first available space not taken by regularly booked shipments—the car may wait for several days on standby basis. Arrangements can be made to have the seller deliver the car to the airline, continuing the car under the seller's insurance. Thus, in case anything should happen before shipment, the seller's insurance takes care of the damage.

As with transport by ship, the cost can either be prepaid or paid after shipment. Shipment by air is faster and appears to be subject to less pilferage. The palletizing and loading of the plane takes less than a day. In order to determine actual cost for your specific car you will have to determine the exact weight (usually taken from the owners manual), then obtain a quote from the shipper, as rates change.

If one of the major carriers flies into your city, then you should have no problem with obtaining freight quotes. However, if none fly into your city, then it is quite possible you may have to fly the car into a nearby major port of entry, and have it trucked to your town, or arrange to have it picked up. If you have the car shipped by boat then you may have to arrange to have it trucked to your town, or arrange to have someone pick it up from the port.

In arranging transportation, insurance will be an integral part of the cost of the transportation. It is suggested that the value of the car for insurance purposes be as close as possible to what its value would be in the United States.

In arranging for transportation from an inland city in the country of origin, such as Frankfurt, be aware that the shipper will have to trans-ship the car to the port where it will be loaded onto a ship. The price for trans-shipment should be included in the shipping fees, together with insurance. If you deliver the car yourself to the port of debarcation, there would be no trans-shipment involved.

Also, be aware that, depending upon the type of easily removed accessories in the car, there will be the possibility of pilferage. It is a good idea to have the radio and other items removed before handing the car over to the shipper. Be sure you have an extra key and don't ship any ownership papers in the car. Also, do not ship any personal items in the car. These will have to be declared to customs and may hold up release of the car.

Check list
- ☐ Waybill
- ☐ Ownership papers
- ☐ CF-7501
- ☐ Bond
- ☐ HS-7 DOT Form
- ☐ 3520-1 EPA Form

220 | 8072 7305   220-8072 7305

Shipper's Name and Address	Shipper's account Number	

Not negotiable
Air Waybill*
(Air Consignment note)
Issued by
Deutsche Lufthansa AG,
D-5000 Köln 21, Von-Gablenz-Straße 2—6

Member of International
Air Transport Association

🛩 **Lufthansa**

Mr. William R. McCreight

West Germany

Copies 1, 2 and 3 of this Air Waybill are originals and have the same validity

Consignee's Name and Address	Consignee's account Number	

Mr. A.L. Smith Jr.

California 95030

U S A

RCVD **LH**

It is agreed that the goods described herein are accepted in apparent good order and condition (except as noted) for carriage subject to the Conditions of Contract on the reverse hereof. The shipper's attention is drawn to the notice concerning carrier's limitation of liability. Shipper may increase such limitation of liability by declaring a higher value for carriage and paying a supplement charge if required.

Issuing Carrier's Agent Name and City

Accounting Information

SFO

Agent's IATA Code	Account No.

Airport of Departure (Addr. of first Carrier) and requested Routing
Issuing Carrier's Agent Name and City

FRANKFURT/MAIN WEST GERMANY

To	By first Carrier	Routing and Destination	to	by	to	by	Currency	CHGS Code	WT/VAL PPD COLL	Other PPD COLL	Declared Value for Carriage	Declared Value for Customs
KFO												

Airport of Destination	Flight/Date	For Carrier Use only	Flight/Date	Amount of Insurance	
SAN FRANCISCO			LH	30.000,—	

INSURANCE — If shipper requests insurance in accordance with conditions on reverse hereof, indicate amount to be insured in figures in box marked amount of insurance

Handling Information

6891 #15

No of Pieces RCP	Gross Weight	kg/lb	Rate Class / Commodity Item No.	Chargeable Weight	Rate / Charge	Total	Nature and Quantity of Goods (incl. Dimensions or Volume)
1	1120,0				4.400,00		dangerous goods as per att. shprs. certification PORSCHE 911 SC 3.0 chassis NR: 911 661 0202 color: white ENGINE #: 6660667

24 70

PAID LUFTHANSA GERMAN AIRLINES

AGT.

Prepaid	Weight Charge	Collect	Other Charges
1722.11			

Valuation Charge

51.19

Insurance premium AWB fee 12,70 handl. 18,50

1773.30

Tax DGR 45,00 85.00 RAF fee 35,00

Total other Charges Due Agent

15

Shipper certifies that the particulars on the face hereof are correct and that insofar as any part of the consignment contains restricted articles, such part is properly described by name and is in proper condition for carriage by air according to the International Air Transport Association's Restricted Articles Regulations.

Total other Charges Due Carrier

1788.30

IMPORT

Signature of Shipper or his Agent

130,80

Total prepaid	Total collect

Currency Conversion Rates	cc charges in Dest. Currency

Executed on _(Date)_ June, 14th 1983 at _(Place)_

Signature of Issuing Carrier or its Agent

For Carriers Use only at Destination	Charges at Destination	Total collect Charges

220-8072 7305

Fahrzeug-Prüfliste
Automobile Inspection Sheet

Lufthansa Cargo

Frachtbrief Nr./AWB No.	von/from	nach/to
220-8012 7305	FRA	SFO

Hersteller/Modell Make and/or model	Kennzeichen/Registration	Farbe/Colour
PORSCHE 911	/	white

Limousine/Sedan ☐

Kabriolett/Convertible ☒

Andere/Others (Jeep, Oldtimer etc.) ☐

Versicherung/Insurance: DELVAG ☒

Andere/Others ☐

Nein/No ☐

Zubehör, Werkzeug und andere Teile des Fahrzeugs bei Übernahme:
Accessories, tools and other parts of vehicle at time of acceptance:

	yes	no		yes	no
Aschenbecher/ash tray	☒	☐	Ersatzreifen/spare tyre	☒	☐
Zigaretten-Anzünder/cig. lighter	☒	☐	Wagenheber/jack	☒	☐
Uhr/clock	☒	☐	Werkzeugkasten/tool kit	☐	☒
Radio ☐ Cass. ☐ TV ☐ CB ☐			Batterie/battery	☒	☐
Sep. Lautspr./sep. loudspeaker	☒	☐	Feuerlöscher/fire extinguisher	☐	☒
Fussmatten/floor mats	☒	☐	Erste Hilfe/first-aid-kit	☒	☐
vorn/front ☐ hinten/rear ☐			Gebrauchsanweisung/Instr. papers	☒	☐
Rückspiegel/rear mirror	☒	☐	Kofferraum leer/trunk empty	☒	☐
Aussenspiegel/outside mirror	☒	☒ 2	Ersatzkanister/spare can	☐	☒
Radio-Antenne/aerial	☐	☒	sichergestellt daß leer/		
Radkappen/hub caps	☐	☒	ensured that empty	☐	☐
Nummernschilder/number plates	☐	☒	Fahrzeug sauber/car clean	☒	☐
Scheibenwischer/windsh. wiper	☒	☐	Anderes/others:		

Folgende Unregelmäßigkeiten wurden bei Übernahme des Fahrzeuges festgestellt:
Following exceptions were noted on this vehicle at time of acceptance:

1. Lackschäden/paint scratches
2. Blechkratzer/metal scratches
3. Blechschäden/dents
4. Glasschäden/glass damages

1 Key

Datum/Date	Achtung/Attention
14.6.83	Werden zusätzlich Autoersatzteile angeliefert, so ist zu überprüfen, ob sie unter die RAR-Bestimmungen fallen.

If additional auto spare parts are delivered, then please check if they are fully within the scope of RAR-regulations.

Remarks

Unterschriften/Signatures:

Absender/Shipper

LH-Agent

LH-Supervisor

1. Original: departure file
2. Duplicate: delivery file

24

ARTHUR J. FRITZ & CO.
CUSTOMHOUSE BROKER & FREIGHT FORWARDER
CONSOLIDATED CARGO — ARRIVAL NOTICE

PLEASE REFER TO THIS REFERENCE NO.	)57-7 ITEM NO: **3**

CONSOLIDATOR	REF.	DATE
DEUGRO/TASP		Oct. 18, 1985

SHIPPER	REF.
DEUGRO, HAMBURG	

CONSIGNEE	NOTIFY
Mrs. Ave # 104 San Mateo CA 94402	Same as consignee

WE ARE PLEASED TO ADVISE YOU OF THE EXPECTED ARRIVAL OF YOUR CONSIGNMENT	FOR PARTICULARS OF DELIVERY APPLY TO:	ARTHUR J. FRITZ & CO. 244 Jackson Street, S.F., CA 94111 Attn: Marilyn Buckley (415) 541-8246 BETWEEN HRS. 9:00-11:00 & 1:00-3:00 ONLY

PORT OF ENTRY	ON/OR ABOUT	B/L NO.
Richmond, CA,	Oct. 24, 1985	3

VESSEL	FROM	ON
AMERICAN HIGHWAY	Emden	Oct. 4, 1985

CLEARANCE SUGGESTIONS

1. Delivery Orders and Customs Permits MUST BE LODGED at the warehouse. Pickup appointment must be prearranged with PASHA TERMINAL, 1311 Canal Blvd., Richmond, CA

2. To make sure that cargo is available, call before pickup.

WAREHOUSE	PHONE
	415 234-8550

B/L DATE	ISSUED AT
Contact: Sue Cochran	

MARKS AND NUMBERS	DESCRIPTION	WEIGHT
NAME: SERIAL NO. 015513	1 Automobile **MB 280 SL**	N/A

CUSTOMS CLEARANCE OPTIONS AVAILABLE - SEE ATTACHED

A.J. Fritz & Co. in possession of original "Intl Zulassungschein" #_________ YES/NO
If yes, International Zulassungschein will be sent to you via registered mail.

OUT OF CONTAINER NO.	N/A

ATTENTION

We will release our DELIVERY ORDER to you, your authorized representative or your Custom House Broker against:

IT IS NOT NECESSARY FOR YOU TO COME TO THE OFFIC ALL PAPERWORK CAN BE DONE BY MAIL. A $25.00 CONSULTATION FEE WILL BE CHARGED ADDITIONALLY FOR ALL VISITS TO THIS OFFICE.

	Surrender of 1 ORIGINAL HOUSE BILL OF LADING XXXXXXXXXXXXXXXXXXXXXXXXXXXXXXXXXXXX
X	XXXXXXXXXXXXXXXX ORIG. DEUGRO TOURIST AUTOMOBILE SHIPPING PROGRAM DOCUMENT
	Your check for charges as per attached Freight Bill — Invoice
X	Payable to Arthur J. Fritz & Co. by CASHIER'S CHECK OR MONEY ORDER ONLY
X	If A.J. Fritz & Co. to make entry all other documents required as per attached. FREE OF ALL CHARGES

YOURS VERY TRULY,

ARTHUR J. FRITZ & CO.

Marilyn Buckley

AJ 155

H. ISERMANN INTERNATIONALE SPEDITION GmbH

Postanschrift / mailing address
Postfach 1251
6457 Maintal 1 / W-Germany

Delivery-address:
Niederlassung / branch office
Nördliche Ladestrasse 145
6000 Frankfurt-Ostgüterbahnhof

Tel: 069/44 80 71
Telex: 414 109 ispe d

Place of Issue: ______________________   Date of Issue: __20.9.85__

For delivery apply to the Clearing Agent listed on the reverse

Port of Destination __SAN FRANCISCO__

Receipt No. ______________________

1 _MB 380 SL (84)_ Plate No. ______________________

Serial No. __WDB107045-1A-015513__

Engine No. ______________   Color: __B.Kurier electr__

Mileage: ______________   Radio Type: __B.Kurier electr__

complete with sparetire, battery, jack/handle, safety-belts, back-uplights, headrests and standard tools

Consignee

SAN MATEO CA 94402   USA

	Floormats	X	Antenna/Aerial		Shelf
X	Warn. Triangle		Luggage Rack		Camp. Equip.
	Warn. Lamp		Spare Gas Can		Tent & Poles
X	First Aid Kit		Tow Rope		Stove & Burner
X	Lighter		Add. Horns	X	**Alloy rims**
	Add. Heater		Foglight front		
	Chrom. Rims		Foglight rear		

The following damages or losses were noted upon acceptance of the car:

	right	left	Other damages or losses
Body, front			
Body, rear			
Bumper, front			
Bumper, rear			
Hood, front			
Hood, rear			
Door			
Fender, front			
Fender, rear			

Transportation from: __Frankfurt__   via: __Emden__   to: __San Francisco__

Conversion Rate US-$ 1.00 = DM ______________   Insurance Value US-$ __27.000,--__

Special Remarks: Conditions of Contract and Clearing Agent are listed on the reverse

FOR CLAIM SETTLEMENT PLEASE FOLLOW THE SPECIAL INFORMATION!

DO NOT LEAVE PERSONAL BELONGINGS IN THE CAR!

Documents received:	Charges:		Prepaid	Collect
International Title	Town-Pickup	US-$/DM		
International Ins. Card	Airport-Pickup	US-$/DM		
Customs Plate Card	Package Price __$ 1.066,--__	US-$/DM		
Export Control Doc.	Road Liability Insurance	US-$/DM		
Export Certificate	Charges as per	US-$/DM		
Invoice Copy	Collection Fee	US-$/DM		
		US-$/DM		
		US-$/DM		
	TOTAL:	US-$/DM		

Receipt issued at __Frankfurt__   car received on ______________________

The undersigned certifies that the particulars hereof are correct and agrees to the ADSp (Allgemeine Deutsche Spediteurbedingungen) and the conditions of carriage of the participating carriers.

We hereby certify that the above mentioned car was received for forwarding by rail, truck, own wheels and/or vessel in forwarder's option in apparent good order and condition, except as noted hereon. We are not responsible for eventual claims which are not detectable upon inspection and/or resulting from defective materials and mechanical defects.

Chapter 4

US Customs requirements

The US Customs Service has the major responsibility to administer the Tariff Act of 1930 (as amended). Its duties include the assessment and collection of all duties, taxes and fees on imported merchandise; enforcement of customs and related laws; and administration of certain navigation laws and treaties. The Customs Service combats smuggling and fraud and enforces regulations of numerous other federal agencies at ports of entry and along the land and sea borders of the United States. Customs is also responsible for enforcing DOT and EPA regulations.

The customs territory of the United States consists of fifty states, the District of Columbia and Puerto Rico. The Customs Service, as an agency under the Department of the Treasury, has its headquarters in Washington, DC, and is headed by the Commissioner of Customs. The field organization consists of seven geographical regions, further divided into districts, with ports of entry within each district. These organizational elements are headed respectively by regional commissioners, district directors (or area directors in the case of the New York region) and port directors. The Customs Service is also responsible for administering the customs laws of the Virgin Islands of the United States.

At the end of this section are an alphabetical list of all ports by state and a list of districts by region. Whenever it is suggested you write to the district or port director for information, the director referred to is the one at the district or port where your goods will enter.

The list is provided so that importation of your auto may be directed to the nearest port of entry. If transport is by ship with final destination to an inland city, the auto may have to be handled several times by one or more carriers. If by air, then it is possible that a single carrier may handle the entire shipment, depending upon destination cities and air rights granted by the United States to the carrier. Additional costs may be involved if shipment is handled by more than one carrier.

Entry process

As the importer of an auto, you will also be the owner of the auto. Your agent, friend, relative or whoever has possession of the auto when shipping it to you (if not yourself) will name you as the consignee on the bill of lading or airbill. If you ship it, then you will name yourself as the consignee on the shipping document.

When a shipment reaches the United States, the consignee files entry documents for the goods with the district or port director at the port of entry. Imported goods are not legally entered until after the shipment has arrived within the port of entry, estimated duties have been paid and delivery of the merchandise has been authorized by customs. It is the responsibility of the importer, you or your agent (which could be a customshouse broker) to arrange for examination and release of the goods.

Goods may enter the country for consumption, for warehousing at the port of arrival, or they may be transported in-bond to another port of entry and enter there under the same conditions as at the port of arrival. Arrangements for transporting the merchandise to an interior port in-bound may be made by the consignee, by a customshouse broker, or by any other person having a sufficient interest in the goods for that purpose. Unless your merchandise arrives directly at the port where you wish to enter it, you may be charged additional fees by the carrier for transportation to that port if other arrangements have not been made.

Goods may be entered by the consignee named in the bill of lading, under which they are shipped, or by the holder of a bill of lading endorsed by the consignee. When the goods are consigned "to order," they may be entered by the holder of the bill of lading properly by the consignor. An airway bill may be used for merchandise arriving by air.

In most instances, entry of an auto is made only by the registered owner for customs purposes. The document issued by the carrier is known as a Carriers Certificate. In certain circumstances, entry may be made by means of a duplicate bill of lading or a shipping receipt. When goods are not imported by a common carrier, possession of the goods at the time of arrival in the United States is sufficient evidence of the right to make entry. (For this reason, *do not* ship the legal papers with the car; send by registered mail to yourself, or carry them with you when you return to the United States.)

The entry of merchandise is a two-part process consisting of (1) filing documents necessary to determine whether merchandise may be released from customs custody and (2) filing documents which contain information for duty assessment and statistical purposes. In certain instances, such as entry of merchandise subject to quotas, all documents must be filed and accepted by customs prior to release of goods.

Within five working days of the date of arrival of a shipment at a US port of entry, documents must be filed at a location specified by the district/area director, unless an extension is granted. These documents include the following:

    a. Entry Manifest (Customs Form 7533) or Application and Special Permit for Immediate Delivery (Customs Form 3461)

    b. Evidence of right to make entry

    c. Commercial invoice or a proforma invoice when the commercial invoice cannot be produced

    d. Packing lists

    e. Other documents necessary to determine merchandise admissibility

If the goods are to be released from customs custody on entry documents, an entry summary for consumption must be filed and estimated duties deposited at the port of entry within ten working days of the time the goods are entered and released.

The entry must be accompanied by evidence that surety (bond) has been obtained to cover the value of the car plus duty. Value must be in US dollars (convert the foreign currency value). Surety usually takes the form of a bond secured by a resident US surety company but may be posted in the form of cash. In the event a customshouse broker is employed for the purpose of making entry, the broker may permit the use of his bond to provide the required coverage.

Following acceptance of the entry, the shipment is examined and released, provided no legal or regulatory violations have occurred. Entry summary documentation is filed, and estimated duties are deposited within ten working days at a designated customshouse after release of the merchandise. Entry summary documentation consists of:

    a. The entry package returned to the importer, broker or an authorized agent after merchandise release is permitted

    b. Entry summary (Customs Form 7501)

    c. Entry record (Customs Form 5101)

    d. HS Form 7, Department of Transportation.

    e. EPA Form 3520-1

    f. Other invoices and documents necessary for assessment of duties, collection of statistics or determination that all import requirements have been satisfied

If there is a failure to file an entry for the goods at the port of entry or port of destination for in-bond shipments within five working days after arrival, the district or port director may place them in a general-order warehouse at the risk and expense of the importer. If the goods are not entered within one year from the date of importation, they can be sold at a public auction. Perishable goods, goods liable to depreciation and explosive substances, however, may be sold immediately.

Storage charges, expense of sale, internal revenue taxes, duties and amounts for the satisfaction of liens must be taken out of the money obtained from the sale of the unentered goods. Any surplus remaining after these deductions is ordinarily payable to the holder of a duly endorsed bill of lading covering the goods. If the goods are subject to internal revenue taxes and will not bring enough on sale at public auction to pay the taxes, they are subject to destruction.

Remember that merchandise arriving in the United States by commercial carrier must be entered by the consignee (importer), his authorized regular employees or the consignee's agent. US customs officers and employees are not authorized to act as agents for importers or forwarders of imported merchandise, although they may give all reasonable advice and assistance to inexperienced importers.

The only persons who are authorized by the tariff laws of the United States to act as agents for importers in the transaction of their customs business are customshouse brokers (private individuals or firms licensed by the Customs Service). Customshouse brokers will prepare and file the necessary customs entries, arrange for payment duties, take steps to effect the release of the goods in customs custody, and otherwise represent their principals in customs matters. The fees charged for these services may vary according to the customshouse broker and the extent of services performed.

It is not necessary that you engage a broker for the purpose of preparing the necessary forms or acting as your agent for importation of your auto. You should be able to do this yourself, thus saving the extra costs, and US customs will accept forms from the importer (you). Many persons using this book have done exactly this.

Key items to have before auto arrives

1. Bond. It is a good idea to obtain the bond prior to the arrival of the auto at the port of entry. The amount of the bond is currently three times the cost of the auto plus the import duty.
2. US customs forms:
   CF-7501 (cashier's copy)
   CF-7501-A (permit copy)
   CF-7501 (salmon-colored copy)
   CF-7501 (control copy)
   CF-7501 (original)
   Bond (single entry bond)
   Invoice (sales receipt for purchase of car)
   Packing List (waybill or airbill from carrier)
   CF-7501 (importer's copy)
   HS-7 (DOT form)
   3520-1 (EPA form)

Most of the data required for the customs forms can be filled-in prior to receipt of the airbill. You should arrange to obtain US customs forms in advance of arrival of auto. In that way time can be saved by having the forms completed before meeting with customs representatives.

3. One gallon of gasoline. This gas is needed in order to get the auto to the nearest gas station; the carrier removes all gasoline (and for ship-ment by boat also disconnects the battery).
4. Information from carrier. In most cases you will be notified by the carrier by either phone or letter. Ask for the following:
   Waybill number (bill of lading, or airbill if by air)
   Date of expected arrival
   Expected time when you can claim your auto
   Costs due upon entry (shipping if not prepaid and any fees for special handling must be paid *prior* to US customs clearance)

After payment of shipping costs, the carrier gives you a copy of the bill of lading (or airbill). The bill of lading or airbill is then used to complete an entry package for submission to US customs.

5. If you do not have a permit to operate your car on the roads of your state when you pick it up from customs, you can obtain a temporary permit from your state department of motor vehicles. Be sure to fully understand all applicable requirements for your particular situation.

Things to do after the auto is released by US customs

1. Take the VIN (vehicle identification number) to State Department of Motor Vehicles (DMV) and apply for registration. In most cases, since you will not have ownership papers (because of using the services of someone to locate and select the car for you), the DMV will not issue permanent papers; you will be issued temporary permits. When ownership papers arrive they will be used to complete vehicle registration. Ownership papers, if not in your possession, should be sent to you, *not* sent with the car.
2. Conformation of auto to EPA and/or DOT requirements (discussed elsewhere).

Entry forms

US customs requires that a specific set of forms be submitted by the importer or his agent in addition to following a prescribed procedure for submission. Goods imported must meet the following criteria:

1. The shipment of goods is imported only for the personal or household use of the importer or his family (an informal entry), which includes gifts, and is not imported for sale or commission. A formal importation is that of an auto for your own use, and brought in under the one-time exemption as allowed by EPA under the law (if not already conformed).

2. Facilities must exist at the place of arrival to permit examination of the shipment by authorized US customs personnel. Inspection and examination must be made prior to release to consignee to ascertain value of the shipment for bonding purposes, duties that may be levied, and other such items that US Customs Service deems appropriate to that particular shipment.

3. The revenue will be adequately protected for the US government.

4. Collateral. US customs requires that some form of collateral be provided by the importer to protect the revenue of the US government from classification errors, clerical errors and so on. One form is a surety, or single entry, bond (CF 7551). Such a bond can be obtained through an insurance agent representing a surety company approved by US customs for this purpose. US customs will usually provide a list of acceptable companies which you may contact.

According to customs regulations, commercial importations valued over $1,000 will not be released from customs custody without the filing of a Customs Entry Bond on which a surety is obligated, or a bond with a cash deposit (or a suitable obligation of the United States) in lieu of surety.

Commercial importation valued over $1,000 not covered by adequate security described above, will be retained in customs' custody at the risk and expense of the importer pending the liquidation of the entry. Liquidation is accomplished on the date the entry is stamped "Liquidated" and the entry is posted on a customs bulletin of entries liquidated, Customs Form 4333.

A single entry surety Bond (CF 7551) is good for only one importation. The bond would be in the amount of the shipment plus the estimated duties and taxes. If the principal is an individual or a partnership, the bond requires two witnesses. If the principal is a corporation, the bond must be signed by one or more officers of the corporation and each signature must be sealed with the corporate seal.

In those cases where an importer chooses to deposit cash in lieu of surety CF 7551, the importer should be aware of the fact that he or she is bound by all conditions of the bond the same as if he or she had received a surety bond. This bond is also good for only one importation. Here, again, if the principal is an individual or a partnership the bond need only have two witnesses. If the principal is a corporation, the bond must be signed by one or more officers of the corporation. The entry should be conspicuously marked to indicate that cash has been deposited in lieu of surety in order to facilitate the refund of the deposit. The cash will be refunded to the principal after liquidation or finalization of the formal entry. Since there is no way to estimate how long the liquidation process will take on a particular entry, there is no way to estimate when the refund will occur. If entered value is $500 or more, the deposit may be held for a minimum of two years after liquidation.

If the importer plans to make commercial importations valued over $1,000 through a particular port on a regular basis, it will alleviate problems and expedite clearance if a term bond (CF 7553) is obtained from an approved surety company. The term bond is valid for one complete year and it eliminates the necessity of getting a single entry bond for each shipment. The minimum amount of a yearly term bond is $10,000.

5. The invoice or bill of sale is that document representing the transaction between you (buyer) or your agent and the seller of the auto. If shipment of the auto is by air, you will probably not have received ownership papers by the time you receive the auto. The papers should be sent (by registered mail) to you and not with the auto—anyone having the papers could claim ownership of the car! In place of the invoice or bill of sale, US customs prescribes a completed proforma invoice. US customs accepts this proxy but, if needed later, may request this invoice to be verified by the copy of the actual papers you receive.

6. The Consumption Entry Form consists of several documents provided by US customs for use in importing the auto and are the forms to be used for that purpose only.

The following is a sample of Customs Form 5106. It is to be completed and submitted at the same time as the first consumption entry is made. This is an informational form and is submitted only once unless there is a change in status or address.

THE DEPARTMENT OF THE TREASURY
Bureau of Customs

(Check Appropriate Box)

Notification of Importer's Number
or
Application for Importer's Number
or
Notice of Change of Name or Address

Customs Form 5106
DEC 69

IRS Employer Number

Suffix

OR IF NO EMPLOYER NUMBER

Social Security No.

FOR CUSTOMS USE ONLY

Customs Serial Number

NAME OF FIRM, AGENCY or
LAST, FIRST and MIDDLE NAME of INDIVIDUAL

STREET ADDRESS

CITY / STATE / ZIP CODE

I CERTIFY THAT: If my IRS Employer Number is used it is correct; that if my Social Security Number is used it is correct and I have no IRS Employer Number; that if neither is used it is because I have neither and my signature constitutes a request for assignment of a Customs Serial Number and an assurance that I have not yet obtained such a number.

DATE

☐ U.S. Government OR;

☐ Principal
☐ Member of Firm
☐ _______________ of the Corporation
(Title)

SIGNATURE

(See Reverse)

FORM APPROVED, BUDGET BUREAU NO. 48-6602

On the next page is a sample of Customs Form 7501. The instructions for preparation of this entry summary form have been edited from the official government form in an effort to help you complete the form.

DEPARTMENT OF THE TREASURY
UNITED STATES CUSTOMS SERVICE

ENTRY SUMMARY

Form Approved OMB No. 1515-0065

1. Entry No.
2. Entry Type Code
3. Entry Summary Date

4. Entry Date
5. Port Code

6. Bond No.
7. Bond Type Code
8. Broker/Importer File No.

9. Ultimate Consignee Name and Address
10. Consignee No.
11. Importer of Record Name and Address
12. Importer No.

13. Exporting Country
14. Export Date

15. Country of Origin
16. Missing Documents

State

17. I.T. No.
18. I.T. Date

19. B/L or AWB No.
20. Mode of Transportation
21. Manufacturer I.D.
22. Reference No.

23. Importing Carrier
24. Foreign Port of Lading
25. Location of Goods/G.O. No.

26. U.S. Port of Unlading
27. Import Date

28. Line No.	30. (A) T.S.U.S.A. No. (B) ADA/CVD Case No.	29. Description of Merchandise 31. (A) Gross Weight (B) Manifest Qty.	32. Net Quantity in T.S.U.S.A. Units	33. (A) Entered Value (B) CHGS (C) Relationship	34. (A) T.S.U.S.A. Rate (B) ADA/CVD Rate (C) I.R.C. Rate (D) Visa No.	35. Duty and I.R. Tax Dollars	Cents

36. Declaration of Importer of Record (Owner or Purchaser) or Authorized Agent

I declare that I am the
☐ importer of record and that the actual owner, purchaser, or consignee for customs purposes is as shown above.

OR

☐ owner or purchaser or agent thereof.

I further declare that the merchandise
☐ was obtained pursuant to a purchase or agreement to purchase and that the prices set forth in the invoice are true.

OR

☐ was not obtained pursuant to a purchase or agreement to purchase and the statements in the invoice as to value or price are true to the best of my knowledge and belief.

I also declare that the statements in the documents herein filed fully disclose to the best of my knowledge and belief the true prices, values, quantities, rebates, drawbacks, fees, commissions, and royalties and are true and correct, and that all goods or services provided to the seller of the merchandise either free or at reduced cost are fully disclosed. I will immediately furnish to the appropriate customs officer any information showing a different state of facts.

Notice required by Paperwork Reduction Act of 1980: This information is needed to ensure that importers/exporters are complying with U.S. customs laws, to allow us to compute and collect the right amount of money, to enforce other agency requirements, and to collect accurate statistical information on imports. Your response is mandatory.

↓ U.S. CUSTOMS USE ↓		TOTALS	
A. Liq. Code	B. Ascertained Duty	37. Duty	
	C. Ascertained Tax	38. Tax	
	D. Ascertained Other	39. Other	
	E. Ascertained Total	40. Total	

41. Signature of Declarant, Title, and Date

Customs Form 7501 (030984)

32

Please note that informal entries previously made on the unnumbered CF 5119A will be made on the CF 7501. The following blocks are to be completed for informal entries where applicable: 1, 2, 5, 11, 12, 13, 15, 17, 18, 19, 23, 27, 28, 29, 30A, 31A, 32, 33A, 34A, 34C, 35, 36, 37, 38, 39, 40, and 41. Each of these block numbers are enclosed in a circle for easy reference.

Block 25, Location of Goods, will be filled in only if merchandise has been placed in a general order warehouse.

1. Entry number

Record the twelve-digit numeric code as follows: the three-digit code assigned to importers and brokers, followed by the last two digits of the fiscal year plus the six-digit entry number and, finally, the one-digit check number. These are preassigned to importers and brokers by customs or may be obtained individually from a customshouse entry unit. (Entry numbers may or may not be used for informal entries.) The acceptable format uses a space between the three parts as follows:
NNN NNNNNNNN N.

NOTE: A new series of eleven-character entry numbers that will incorporate a three-character importer/broker filer code is planned. Until this series is adopted (and due to space limitations on the form), the existing three-character importer/broker code numbers shall be recorded outside of and immediately to the left of block #1, as shown here:

	1. Entry No.
NNN	NNNNNNNN N

2. Entry type code

Record the appropriate entry type code by selecting from the following chart the two-digit code for the type of entry summary being filed. The first digit of the code identifies the general category of the entry (i.e., consumption, 0; informal, 1; warehouse, 2). The second digit further defines the specific processing type within the entry category (i.e., quota, 2; free and dutiable, 1). If a transaction requires the use of more than one entry type code, the special entry processing type code 99 should be used.

Code	Entry type
	Consumption entries
01	Free and dutiable
02	Quota
03	Countervailing/antidumping duty
04	Appraisement
05	Vessel repair
06	Foreign trade zone (consumption)
07	Quota and ADD/CVD combinations
	Informal entries
11	Free and dutiable
12	Quota
	Warehouse entries
21	Warehouse
22	Rewarehouse
23	Temporary importation bond
24	Trade fair
25	Permanent exhibition
26	Foreign trade zone (admission)
	Warehouse withdrawal
31	For consumption
32	Quota
33	Aircraft and vessel supply (immediate export)
34	Countervailing and antidumping duty
35	For transportation
36	For immediate exportation
37	For transportation and exportation
38	General order
39	Quota and ADD/CVD combinations
	Drawback entries
41	Manufacturer
42	Same condition
43	Rejected importation
	Government entries
51	Defense contract importation (DCASR)
52	Dutiable
53	Free
	Transportation entries
61	Immediate transportation
62	Transportation and exportation
63	Immediate exportation
64	Barge movement
65	Permit to proceed
66	Baggage
	Special processing entries
99	Special entry processing

3. Entry summary date

This block is to record the date the entry summary or entry/entry summary is filed (six-digit numeric code showing month, day, year (MMDDYY; slashes, dashes and spaces may be used). The preparer will record the import specialist team designation in the upper right portion of this block (three-digit numeric code).

4. Entry date

Record the six-digit numeric code: month, day, year (MMDDYY; slashes, dashes and spaces may be used). Normally, it is the date the goods are released, except for immediate delivery, quota goods or when the importer/broker requests another date prior to release (see Customs Form 19 CFR 141.68).

5. Port code

Record the four-digit numeric code of the port where the merchandise was entered under an entry or immediate delivery permit. Port codes are to be found in Annex A of the Tariff Schedule of the United States Annotated (TSUSA). The port code should be entered with no spaces or hyphens.

6. Bond number

Record the three-digit numeric code that identifies the surety company on the bond. The code number is obtained from the ADP report entitled Surety Master File, which is updated periodically. For US government importations and other entry types not requiring surety (except informal entries), the code 999 should appear in this block.

NOTE: This block is intentionally labeled Bond Number rather than Surety Code Number. Bond numbers unique to each surety will be recorded here.

7. Bond type code

Record the single-digit numeric code as applicable, according to the following list.

0 US government
1 Single entry
2 Consumption (for a one-year term)
3 Temporary importation term (for a temporary term, usually less than one year)
4 Vessel term (a special bond for goods arriving on a certain vessel)
5 General term (for general terms)
6 Drawback (ensures you can get your money back if the bond is not used, or if you have an account with US customs, in which case you are constantly bringing goods into and out of the United States)
8 Continuous (ensures that you do not have to renew the bond at the end of the period; it automatically renews)*
9 Single entry (used by owner who wishes to import his own vehicle)*

These types of bonds relate to the Revised Customs Bond Structure and will be used upon implementation of that system.

8. Broker/importer file number

This block is reserved for a broker's or importer's internal file or reference number.

9. Ultimate consignee name and address

Record the name and address (including postal code, if any) of the individual or firm for whose account the merchandise is imported (if same as importer of record, leave blank). Also enter the US Postal Service's standard two-letter state or territory abbreviation in the space provided to identify the ultimate consignee state. If entry summary represents a consolidated shipment, leave blank (but record "US" in the state code block). If the ultimate consignee is located in a foreign nation, record "FN" as state abbreviation.

10. Consignee number

Record the IRS number, customs-assigned number or Social Security number of the consignee (not required if it is the same as importer of record). For consolidated shipments, enter zeros.

Only the following formats shall be used:

IRS number or consolidated shipments	NN-NNNNNNN
IRS number with suffix	NN-NNNNNNNXX
Customs-assigned number	NNNN-NNNNN
Social Security number	NNN-NN-NNNN

11. Importer of record name and address

Record the name and address (including postal code) of the importer of record. This is the individual or firm liable for payment of all duties and meeting all statutory and regulatory requirements incurred as a result of importation.

12. Importer number

Record the IRS number, customs-assigned number, or Social Security number of the importer of record. (For format, see instructions above for Consignee number.)

13. Exporting country

Record the exporting country utilizing ISO Alpha-2 country codes specified in the International Standard ISO 3166.

The country of exportation is usually the country of origin, except when the merchandise while located in a third country is the subject of a new purchase. In this event, the third country shall be regarded as the country of export (see Customs Form 19 CFR 152.33).

For merchandise entering the US customs territory from a US foreign trade zone, leave blank.

For multiple countries of export, enter "multi" in this block, and associate the country of export with each line item (or where line items are segregated by invoice, associate with each invoice) in column 28 prefixed with an E, or place on a separate attachment, or record in block 29 as part of the description.

14. Export date

For merchandise exported by vessel, record the month, day, year on which the carrier departed the last port in the exporting country (MMDDYY; slashes, dashes and spaces may be used).

For merchandise exported by air, record the month, day, year in which the aircraft departed the last airport in the exporting country (MMDDYY; slashes, dashes and spaces may be used).

For overland shipments from Canada or Mexico and shipments where the port of lading is located outside the exporting country (e.g., goods are exported from Switzerland but laden and shipped from Hamburg, West Germany), record the month, day, year in which the goods crossed the border of the exporting country (Switzerland in this example. MMDDYY; slashes, dashes and spaces may be used).

For mail shipments, record the date of export as noted on Customs Form 3509, Notice to Addressee (MMDDYY; slashes, dashes and spaces may be used).

For goods entering the US customs territory from a US foreign trade zone, leave blank.

For multiple dates of export, enter "multi" in this block, and associate the date of export with each line item (or where line items are segregated by invoice, associate with each invoice) in block 28, or place on a separate attachment, or record in block 29 as a part of the description.

15. Country of origin

Record the country of origin utilizing the ISO country codes specified in International Standard ISO 3166.

The country of origin is the country of manufacture, production or growth of any article. Further work or material added to an article in another country must effect a substantial transformation in order to render such other country the country of origin.

When merchandise is invoiced in or exported from a country other than that in which it originated, the actual country of origin shall be specified rather than the country of invoice or exportation.

When a single entry summary covers merchandise from more than one country of origin, enter "multi" in this block and in column 28, directly below the line number, indicate a separate ISO code for the country of origin corresponding to each line item.

16. Missing documents

Record the appropriate document code number(s) to indicate documents not available at the time of filing the entry summary, using the following codes:

01 Commercial invoice
02 Form A
03 CF 3311
04 Assembly declaration [19 CFR 10.24 (a)(1)]
05 Declaration of foreign shipper (19 CFR 10.1, 10.9(e), 10.84)
06 Importer declaration (19 CFR 10.9(f), 10.24(a)(2), 10.84)
07 Repair affidavit (19 CFR 10.8)
08 CF 4455
09 CF 3321 (19 CFR 10.43, 10.44, 10.52, 10.75)
10 CF 5523 (19 CFR 141.89)
11 CF 3291 (19 CFR 12.41)
12 Original manufacturer's purchase order [19 CFR 10.84(c)]
13 Artist's declaration [19 CFR 10.48 (b)(1)]
14 Lease statement [19 CFR 10.108(b)]
15 Re-Melting certificate [19 CFR 54.6(a)]
16 Corrected commercial invoice (19 CFR 141.89, et al)
17 Other agency forms (19 CFR Part 12)
18 Duty-free entry certificate (19 CFR 10.101, 832.00 TSUSA)
19 to 98 – Reserved
99 If three or more documents are missing, record the code number for the first document and insert code "99" for the second and any additional documents.

If a document has been waived prior to entry summary filing, do not record that document as missing.

17. I.T. number

Record the In Transit (IT) Entry Number (CF 7512). If multiple, place additional ITs on a separate attachment associated with each line item (or where line items are segregated by invoice, associate with each invoice) or across lines 30 to 32 associated with each line item (or invoice).

18. I.T. date

Record the date of the In Transit Entry (CF 7512) (MMDDYY; slashes, dashes and spaces may be used). If multiple, place additional dates on separate attachment associated with each line item (or where line items are segregated by invoice, associate with each invoice) or across lines 30 to 32 associated with each line item (or invoice).

19. Bill of lading or air waybill number

Record the number assigned on the manifest by the international ocean or air carrier delivering the goods to the United States. For imports by means other than sea or air, leave blank.

If multiple, list additional numbers across the top of columns 30 to 32 or on a separate attachment.

20. Mode of transportation

Record the method of transportation by which the imported merchandise entered the first US port, utilizing the following two-digit numeric codes:

10 Vessel, non-container, including all cargo at first US port of unlading aboard a vessel regardless of later disposition; lightered, land bridge and LASH (a certain type of barge) included. If container status unknown but goods did arrive by vessel, use this code.

11 Vessel, container
20 Rail
30 Road (including all cargo via highway. Foot-borne and animal-borne are considered road)
40 Air
50 Mail
60 Not used at this time
70 Fixed transport installation (includes pipeline, powerhouse, etc.)
80 Not used at this time

For merchandise arriving in the US customs territory from a US foreign trade zone, leave blank.

21. Manufacturer identification

This block is provided to accommodate a future reporting requirement. Manufacturers will be identified by their telex number or, if not available, their telephone number. Country codes used in conjunction with telex and telephone numbers (manufacturer's number) will then uniquely identify each foreign firm.

22. Reference number

Record the IRS number, customs-assigned number or Social Security number of the individual or firm to whom refunds, bills or notices of extension or suspension of liquidation are to be sent (if other than importer of record and if CF 4811 is on file). Use same format as consignee number.

23. Importing carrier

For merchandise arriving in the US by vessel, record the name of the vessel which transported the merchandise from the foreign port of lading to the first US port of unlading. Vessel identifier codes that are currently acceptable to the Bureau of the Census may be recorded in lieu of vessel name.

For merchandise arriving in the US by air, record the IATA code corresponding to the name of the airline which transported the merchandise from the last airport of foreign lading to the first US airport of unlading. Use the two-digit alpha code for each airline as listed in the International Air Carriers Guide (it is anticipated that the IATA codes for airlines will become three digits in 1987).

For merchandise arriving in the United States by means of transportation other than by vessel or air, leave blank.

Do not record the name of a domestic carrier transporting merchandise after initial lading in the United States.

For merchandise arriving in the US customs territory from a US foreign trade zone, insert "FTZ" followed by the FTZ number.

24. Foreign port of lading

For merchandise arriving in the United States by vessel, record the five-digit numeric code listed in the Department of Commerce Schedule K for the foreign port at which the merchandise was actually laden on the vessel that carried the merchandise to the US. If the foreign port of lading is not provided for by name in Schedule K, use the code for "all other ports" for the port of foreign lading for that country.

For merchandise entering the US customs territory from a US foreign trade zone, leave blank.

When a single entry summary covers merchandise laden at more than one foreign port, enter multi in this block, and record the foreign port of lading separately in the Line Number column directly below the line number for each line item (or group of line items if segregated by invoice) for the merchandise laden at each foreign port (where there are multiple ports of lading and also multiple countries of origin, see instructions under Country of origin, block 15. If both code numbers will be required for one line item, place the country of origin code directly below the line number and place the port of lading code directly under the country of origin code).

If merchandise is transported by a mode of transportation other than vessel, leave blank.

25. Location of goods/G.O. number

Where the entry summary serves as entry/entry summary, record the pier or site where the goods are available for examination. For air shipments, record the flight number. If the firm's codes are available they may be used instead of pier or site.

In the case of merchandise placed in a general order (G.O.) warehouse, record the number assigned by customs.

In the case of goods placed in a bonded warehouse, record the name of the bonded warehouse where the goods will be delivered (or record the customs-assigned number for the bonded warehouse, when available).

In the case where the entry summary serves as warehouse entry/entry summary, record the pier or site where the goods are available for examination followed by the name of the bonded warehouse where the goods will be delivered (or the customs-assigned number).

26. US port of unlading

For merchandise imported by vessel or air, record the four-digit numeric TUSA Schedule D code which identifies the US port at which the merchandise was unladen from the importing vessel or aircraft.

For merchandise arriving in the United States by means of transportation other than vessel or air, leave blank.

For merchandise arriving in the US customs territory from a US foreign trade zone, leave blank.

27. Import date

For merchandise arriving in the United States by vessel, record the month, day, year (MMDDYY; slashes, dashes and spaces may be used) in which the importing vessel transporting the merchandise from the foreign country arrived within the limits of the US port with the intent to unlade.

For merchandise arriving in the United States other than by vessel, record the month, day, year (MMDDYY; slashes, dashes and spaces may be used) in which the merchandise arrived within the limits of the United States.

For merchandise arriving in the US customs territory from a US foreign trade zone, leave blank.

28. Line number

Record the appropriate line item number, in sequence, beginning with the number 001.

A "line item" refers to a commodity from one country, covered by a line which includes a net quantity, entered value, TSUSA number, CHGS, and rate of duty and tax. However, some line items may actually include more than one TSUSA number and value. For example, many items found in Schedule 8 require a dual TSUSA number. Articles assembled abroad with American components require TSUSA number 807.00 along with the appropriate Schedule 1 through 7 TSUSA number. Also, for certain steel products, there are additional duties for chromium, molybdenum, tungsten and vanadium content which require that the individual TSUSA item numbers for these extra duties be reported in addition to the base TSUSA item number for the iron or steel product containing these alloys. In those cases where two or more TSUSA item numbers are required to be shown for a commodity, these dual reporting numbers shall be treated as one line number.

For multiple elements in blocks 13, 14, 15 and 24, see specific instructions for those items.

29. Description of merchandise

A description of the articles in sufficient detail to permit the classification thereof under the proper statistical reporting number in the TSUSA should be reported in numbers 30 to 32. The standard definitions from the TSUSA tape extracts from the TSUSA data base are acceptable for this requirement.

30. A. TSUSA number

Record the appropriate duty/statistical reporting number under which the article is classified in the Tariff Schedules of the United States Annotated (use of decimal points after the first three digits of the TSUSA number is optional).

If more than one TSUSA number is required, follow the reporting instructions in the statistical headnotes in the appropriate TSUSA schedule, part or subpart.

When Generalized System of Preferences (GSP) is claimed, precede the TSUSA number with the letter A. (GSP refers to duty-free treatment of third-world countries.) When Carribean Basin Initiative Participants (CBI) is claimed, precede the TSUSA number with the letter C. (CBI refers to residents of the Carribean eligible for the plan.) When a claim is made in accordance with General Headnote 3(a), precede the TSUSA with the letter I. When Folklore is claimed, precede the TSUSA number with the letter F. (Folklore means traditional goods made by a people, such as hats made by Chinese; easily recognizable. It does not apply in any way to vehicles.)

B. Antidumping/countervailing duty case number

Record, directly below the TSUSA number, the appropriate antidumping/countervailing duty case number(s) as assigned by the Department of Commerce, International Trade Administration. The following formats shall be used: A-000-000-000 (ADA), C-000-000-000 (CVD).

Where space only permits twelve characters, use the following formats: A000-000-000 (ADA), C000-000-000 (CVD).

When bonding is permitted, in parentheses, record the bond number.

31. A. Gross weight

Record the gross shipping weight in pounds for articles imported in vessels or aircraft (do not report gross weight for merchandise arriving in the United States by other modes of transportation). The gross weight must be reported on the same line with the entered value (33A). Supply separate gross weight information for each item number. If the gross weight is not available for each number, approximate shipping weight for each item shall be estimated and reported. The total of these estimated weights should equal the actual gross shipping weight. For multiline summaries, the total gross weight need not be shown at all.

In the case of containerized cargo carried in lift vans, cargo vans or similar substantial outer containers, the weight of such containers should not be included in the gross weight of the merchandise covered by each line item.

B. Manifest quantity

This space is provided to accommodate a future reporting requirement. The instruction will be to enter the manifest quantity and unit.

32. Net quantity in TSUSA units

When a unit of quantity is specified in the TSUSA for the item number, report the net quantity in the specified unit, and show the unit after the net quantity figure.

Record quantities in whole units unless fractions of units are required for other customs purposes. When expressing fractions, decimals only shall be used.

If no unit of quantity is specified in the TSUSA for the item number, leave blank.

If two units of quantity are shown for the item number in the TSUSA, report the net quantity for both with the unit of quantity indicated in each case. Insert the quantity in terms of the unit marked in the TSUSA with a V on the line with the entered value. Put the quantity in terms of any other unit below the first quantity and enclose it in parentheses. Example: Shipment consists of 50 dozen all-white

T-shirts, weighing two pounds per dozen and valued at $10 per dozen. Report as follows:

Block 30	Block 31	Block 32	Block 33
379.401D	100 lbs	V600 (50 doz.)	500

33. A. Entered value

Record the US dollar value in accordance with the definition in Section 402, Tariff Act of 1930, as amended (19 USC 1402) for all merchandise.

This value shall be shown for each TSUSA item number on the same line with the item number where a value is required.

Report the value in whole dollars rounded off to the nearest whole dollar. Dollar signs shall be omitted.

B. Charges (CHGS)

In accordance with TSUSA general statistical headnote 1 (a)(xvi), record the aggregate cost (not including US import duty, if any) in US dollars of freight, insurance and all other costs, charges and expenses incurred in bringing the merchandise from alongside the carrier at the foreign port of lading in the exporting country and placing it alongside the carrier at the first US port of entry.

This value shall be shown for each TSUSA item number beneath the entered value and identified with the letter C (e.g. C550).

Charges are not required for line items under $250 or on informal entries.

Record the value in whole dollars rounded off to the nearest whole dollar. Dollar signs shall be omitted.

In the case of overland shipments (i.e., merchandise transported to the United States by means other than vessel or air) originating in Canada or Mexico, expenses incurred in transporting merchandise beyond the Canada-US or Mexico-US borders, by means other than vessel or air (i.e., overland by automobile, truck, train, pipeline, parcel post or mail), leave blank.

C. Relationship

Record whether the transaction was between related parties as defined by Section 402(g)(l) of the Tariff Act of 1930, as amended, by placing a Y in the column for related and an N for not related. (The words "related" and "not related" also may be used.)

Y or N may be recorded once, at the top of column 33, when applicable to the entire transaction or may be recorded with each line item below entered value and charges. Y or N must be recorded with each line item when the relationship differs for line items.

34. A. TSUSA rate

Record the rate(s) of duty for the classified item as designated in the TSUSA: free, ad valorem, specific or compound.

B. Antidumping/countervailing duty rate

Record the antidumping and/or countervailing duty rate(s) as designated by the Department of Commerce, International Trade Administration, directly opposite the respective ADA/CVD case number(s) shown in column 30.

Where bonding is permitted, record the rate(s) in column 34 as indicated above but in parentheses, in column 33, record the word "bonded" and record *no amount* in column 35.

C. IRC rate

Record the tax rate(s) for the classified item as designated in the TSUSA.

If IR tax is deferred, precede IRC rate with "def." Show the amount in column 35 and in block 38 but do not include in the total for block 40.

D. VISA number

Record the letter V followed by the visa number for each line of merchandise as it appears on the invoice. Visa numbers may currently be up to nine alpha/numeric characters. Standardization is planned.

In the event there is any other charge or exaction (e.g., fees) not enumerated above, record the rate in this column and identify each charge or exaction immediately to the left of such rate.

35. Duty and IR tax

Record the estimated TSUSA antidumping or countervailing duty, IR tax, and any other charges calculated by applying the rate times the dutiable value or quantity. The amount shown in this column must be directly opposite the appropriate TSUSA, antidumping, countervailing duty rate, IR rate and other charges (except where bonding is permitted for antidumping or countervailing duty; in that case, leave blank. See instructions under column 34 A.). Dollar signs shall be omitted.

36. Declaration

Read the information carefully and check the appropriate boxes.

37. Duty

Record the total estimated duty paid (excluding antidumping or countervailing duty).

When the entry summary consists of more than one page, record on the first page the total estimated duty paid.

38. Tax

Record the total estimated tax paid, including any amount deferred. When the entry summary consists of more than one page, record on the first page the total estimated tax paid.

39. Other

Record the total estimated antidumping or countervailing duties or other charges or exactions paid. When the entry summary consists of more than one page, record on the first page the total amount of antidumping or countervailing duties or other charges or exactions paid.

40. Total
Record the sum of blocks 37, 38 and 39, not including any deferred tax shown in column 35 and block 38 or antidumping or countervailing duty which has been bonded for.

41. Signature of declarant, title and date
Record the signature of the declarant, the job title of the owner, purchaser or agent who signs the declaration, and the month, day and year when the declaration is signed.

When the entry summary consists of more than one page, the signature of the declarant, title and date must be recorded on the first page.

Facsimile signatures are acceptable when prior approval has been obtained from the district, area or port director.

Summary of entered value/currency conversion
The summary of entered value and currency conversion (if appropriate) may be shown on a worksheet attached to the entry summary or across columns 30 and 31 just above block 36. On a multipage entry summary, show the summary of entered values on the last page following the last line item.

Accelerated drawback
When filing a drawback claim on a drawback form not yet revised, include the former entry record (CF 5101) data by filing with the drawback entry submission two copies of CF 7501.

Only the following data need be shown as appropriate (block numbers appear in parentheses): entry number (1), entry type code (2), entry date (4), bond number (6), bond type code (7), consignee number (10), importer number (12), duty (37), I.R. tax (38), total (40), reference number (22).

All information above pertains to the drawback entry being filed.

Appraisement entry
When CF 7501 is used as an appraisement entry, the same declaration which now appears on CF 7500, requesting appraisement under Section 498(a) of the Tariff Act of 1930, as amended, should be added to the body of CF 7501 or stapled on top of it in the left margin as follows:

I hereby request appraisement under Section 498(a), Tariff Act of 1930, as amended. I declare, to the best of my knowledge and belief, that this entry and the documents presented therewith set forth all the information in my possession, or in the possession of the owner of the merchandise described herein, as to the cost of such merchandise; that I am unable to obtain any further information as to the value of the said merchandise or to determine its value for the purpose of making formal entry thereof; that the information contained in this entry and in the accompanying documents is true and correct; and that the person(s) named above is the owner of the same merchandise.

Signature ___________________________________

Title ___________________________________

To the District Director: The merchandise described above has been examined and the contents and values are noted above.

Examiner ___________________________________

Date ___________________________________

Customs Officer ___________________________________

Date ___________________________________

Permit copy
When the entry summary serves as the entry/entry summary, an additional copy of CF 7501 will be provided. The additional copy will be prominently marked permit, in red ink, by means of a stamp. The stamp will be in block letters and at least three inches by one inch. The CF 7501 will be stamped in the center of the body of the form. All appropriate CF 7501 information should be provided.

Multiple data elements
Except where specific instructions provide, where a data block will involve more than one data element, enter "multi" and identify and list the data elements on a separate attachment of CF7501, or where room permits, in the body of CF 7501 or continuation sheet and associate with the appropriate line item (or where line items are segregated by invoice, associate with each invoice).

Delimiters for line items
Each line item on CF 7501 and continuation sheet must be separated by a solid line, broken line or a space to facilitate the processing of the entry summary.

Additional data elements
Filers of CF 7501 may, on their own initiative, provide additional or clarifying information on the form, provided such additional information does not interfere with the reporting of those required data elements. Such addi-

tional or clarifying information may be placed in any location on the form solely at the discretion of the filer, provided it does not interfere with any required data element. In this case, the Customs Service will not mandate either what additional information may be on the form or where it is to be placed.

Invoices may be separately identified in the body of CF 7501 and the continuation sheet across columns 30 to 35 followed by the line items appropriate to that invoice.

The following information is intended to be of value to an importer unfamiliar with the procedures of filing a formal entry, and is condensed to the essentials, and is not necessarily in order of importance.

A Formal Entry is required on commercial shipments with foreign value in excess of $1,000 and may be required on other shipments at the direction of the US Customs Service.

The carrier will notify the consignee upon arrival of the merchandise into the United States. Charges by the carrier must be paid prior to customs clearance. Transport of the merchandise to the importer's premises is the responsibility of the importer.

Upon receipt of a completely filled-in invoice from the exporter (supplier), the importer (or representative) should ascertain from the US Customs Service facility the classification and assignment of a TSUSA number, and rate of duty for same.

After the merchandise has been classified and noted by a commodity specialist, the Consumption Entry package consisting of the necessary forms may be filled in on typewriter or printed legibly in ink using carbon paper between the sheets. (If filled in with pen, use black or dark blue ink only.) Basically, the information required on this set of forms is obtained from the invoice, the bill of lading and/or notification of mail shipment forms covering the shipment. The package consists of the following forms:

    a. Single Entry Bond

    b. Invoice: Must show name of seller, name of buyer, date of transaction, description of merchandise in English and amount of transaction in US dollars.

    c. Bill of Lading or "Notice of Addressee of Arrival of Mail Shipment" (CF3509).

    d. Consumption Entry (CF 7501): Need original and three (3) copies, plus yellow-colored statistical copy and one (1) copy of 7501 marked Permit.

Next in the procedure is to acquire a single entry bond from an insurance agent representing a surety company approved by US customs. A single entry bond covers a single importation and must be equal to the domestic value of the shipment plus the duty and IR tax if any applies. The primary purpose of the bond is to protect the revenue of the US government from classification errors, clerical errors and so on. Other types of bonds are available if you will be importing regularly.

Department of the Treasury
U.S. Customs Service

ENTRY RECORD

Customs Form 5101 (9-9-77)

WAS SHIPMENT CONTAINERIZED [ ] YES

FORM APPROVED
9. No. 48-R0255

1. ENTRY CODE

2. BOND CODE

3. IMPORTER OF RECORD NUMBER*

Importer Number of Individual or firm whose name appears as Importer of Record on entry.

ENTRY CODES
1. Consumption Dutiable
2. Vessel Repair
3. Appraisement
4. Warehouse
5. Drawback
6. Bonded A/C Fuel
7. Consumption Free

BOND CODES
1. Single Entry (any type)
2. CF 7553 (Consump. Term)
3. CF 7563 A (Temp. Imp.)
4. CF 7569 (Vessel Term)
5. CF 7595 (General Term)
6. CF 7611 (Drawback Term)

4. ULTIMATE CONSIGNEE NUMBER*

Importer Number of Individual or firm whose name appears as the Ultimate Consignee on entry. If more than one owner of merchandise enter word "consolidated".

5a. DATE OF ENTRY

5b. ENTRY NUMBER

6. REFERENCE NUMBER*

Importer Number of Individual or firm to whom Refund, Bills or Notices of Liquidation are to be sent if other than Importer of Record.

7. DUTY
$

8. I.R. TAX
$

*(Show hyphens as appropriate.)

9. SURETY CODE

10. DESCRIPTION OF MERCHANDISE

11. PORT CODE

12. MISSING DOCUMENTS

LIQUIDATOR CODE
(Customs Use Only)

I HEREBY make application to make entry prior to production of missing document(s) named above. S

(Original)

Instructions for completing entry record (CF 5101)

1.	Entry Code:	If dutiable, enter 1; if free of duty, enter 7.
2.	Bond Code:	If single entry bond, enter 1.
3.	Importer of Record No.:	Use importer's IRS number or Social Security number. If importer has neither, customs will assign one.
4.	Ultimate Consignee:	Same as above; you may enter same.
5a.	Date of Entry:	Today's date (date of entry submission).
5b.	Entry Number:	Number assigned by customs and used on CF 7501.
6.	Reference Number:	May be left blank.
7.	Duty:	Amount of duty paid on Entry. If duty free, enter two zeros.
8.	I.R. Tax:	Amount of Internal Revenue Tax (if applicable).
9.	Surety Code No.:	Same three-digit number used on CF 7501.
10.	Description of Merchandise:	Number of cartons and brief description of goods.
	Team Number:	Digit number of commodity team specialist which handles this merchandise.
11.	Port Code:	For airport, enter 2801; for surface, enter 2809.
12.	Missing Documents:	Leave blank, unless a bond has been posted for the production of a required document.

Notes: The importer's reference number is optional, for your convenience. You can note it in the upper left-hand corner of the form. The importer's name is also optional, but please show "303" in the upper right-hand corner. This denotes an individual. Leave the signature line blank, unless a bond has been posted for the production of a required document.

INFORMATION
NOTICE

NUMBER: 86-05

ISSUE DATE: October 2, 1985

EXPIRES:

SUBJECT: New Single-Entry Bond Requirements for Non-Conforming Vehicles

Non-conforming vehicles are conditionally prohibited merchandise. Such merchandise entered or withdrawn from warehouse on or after November 1, 1985 must be covered by a Single-Entry Bond equal to three times the total foreign value of the article. This total value shall include any modifications or conversions abroad. For example, a car purchased for $10,000 in Europe with an additional $5,000 in modification costs abroad would require a bond for $45,000 ($15,000 x 3).

Importers are reminded of their obligations under the bond; Customs must obtain clearances from BOTH the Environmental Protection Agency (EPA) and the Department of Transportation (DOT) within 180 days from the date of entry. If Customs has not received timely notices of compliance from both agencies Customs will issue a notice of Redelivery/Liquidated Damages at the close of that period. If the importer fails to redeliver, destroy or export the car within the time permitted, Customs shall demand liquidated damages in the full amount of the bond.

Paul R. Andrews
District Director

Customs Form 232-E (01-22-80)

IMMEDIATE DELIVERY AND CONSUMPTION ENTRY BOND (Single Entry)

(To redeliver merchandise, to produce documents, to perform conditions of release, such as to label, hold for inspection, set-up etc. to be taken in all cases when release is requested prior to inspection, examination, or liquidation)

Know All Men by These Presents That* ___A. LAWRENCE SMITH JR.___________________________

____,

of ____ , as principal,

and* ___THE . INSURANCE COMPANY_______________ , of ____,

and ___San Francisco, CA 94105_______________ , of ____,

as sureties, are held and firmly bound unto the UNITED STATES OF AMERICA in the sum of ___THIRTEEN THOUSAND AND NO/100

____ dollars ($ __13,000.00___),

for the payment of which we bind ourselves, our heirs, executors, administrators, successors, and assigns, jointly and severally, firmly by these presents.

WITNESS our hands and seals this ___________14th___________ day of ___June___________, 19 _83_

WHEREAS, certain merchandise, in whole or in part, may be entered under the provisions of section 484, Tariff Act of 1930, as amended, and duties deposited under the provisions of section 505 (a), Tariff Act of 1930, as amended; or

WHEREAS, certain articles described in an application dated _______________________, 19 ________, for special permit to land and deliver immediately are expected to arrive at the port of ___SAN FRANCISCO_______________________,

from ___FRANKFURT, GERMANY___________,on ___AIRCRAFT_______________, and the immediate delivery of such article is necessary; and
(Vessel, vehicle, or aircraft)

WHEREAS, pursuant to regulations promulgated under the provisions of section 448 (b), Tariff Act of 1930, the above-bounden principal desires the release of the articles described in the application prior to the making of an entry therefor and the payment of duties thereon; or

WHEREAS, certain articles have been imported at the port of ______SAN FRANCISCO_______________, and entered at

said port for consumption on entry No. _______________, dated _______________, 19 _______, and described therein; and

WHEREAS, the above-bounden principal may request that the merchandise be examined elsewhere than at the public store, wharf, or other place in charge of a customs officer; and

WHEREAS, the above-bounden principal desires release of the articles described in the permit or entry prior to the ascertainment by customs officers of the quantity and value of such articles, and of the full amount of the duties and charges due thereon, and prior to the decision by the proper officer as to the right of the articles to admission into the United States;

NOW, THEREFORE, THE CONDITION OF THIS OBLIGATION IS SUCH THAT—

(1) The above-bounden principal, in consideration of the release of all or any part of the shipment covered by the entry specified above before the full amount of duties and taxes imposed upon or by reason of importation has been finally determined, and notwithstanding section 485 (d), Tariff Act of 1930, or any other provisions of law, voluntarily undertakes and agrees to pay any and all such duties and taxes found to be due on the shipment referred to, but not in excess of the amount of this bond, upon condition that no other provision of this bond shall be invoked for the purpose of enforcing the collection of such duties and taxes and upon the further condition that this obligation to pay any and all such duties and taxes found to be due on the shipment (not exceeding the amount of this bond) shall become null and void and of no force and effect on and after the date on which the abovebounden principal files with the district director in the manner and within the time prescribed by the regulations a superseding bond on customs Form 7601 of the owner whose declaration has been filed in accordance with the provisions of said section 485 (d), in which bond the owner undertakes and agrees to pay any and all such duties and taxes found due on the shipment covered by the above-mentioned entry;

(2) (a) If, where entry is made pursuant to section 484, Tariff Act of 1930, as amended, the above-bounden principal, within the time prescribed in the Customs regulations shall file with the appropriate customs officer the documentation required by the Customs

If the principal or surety is a corporation, the name of the State in which incorporated also shall be shown.

regulations to enable Customs to (1) determine whether the merchandise may be released from Customs custody, (2) properly assess duties on the merchandise, (3) collect accurate statistics with respect to the merchandise, and (4) determine whether applicable requirements of law or regulation are met; and if the above-bounden principal, within the time prescribed in the Customs regulations, shall deposit the duties and taxes imposed upon or by reason of importation estimated to be due thereon; or if, in the event of failure to file the documentation or to deposit duties and taxes, he shall pay to the district director of Customs as liquidated damages an amount equal to the value of the merchandise as to which there shall have been default plus the duties and taxes thereon (it being understood and agreed that the amount to be collected shall be based upon the quantity and value of the merchandise as determined by the district director, and that the decision of the district director as to the status of the merchandise, whether free or dutiable, together with the rate and amount of duties and taxes, also shall be binding on all parties to this obligation);

(2) (b) If, in cases where the merchandise has been released prior to entry pursuant to section 448 (b) of the tariff act, the above-bounden principal within the time prescribed in Customs regulations of 1943, as amended, after the release of the articles described in the application for a special permit, shall make entry for such articles and deposit the duties and taxes imposed upon or by reason of importation estimated to be due thereon; or if, in the event of failure to make entry or to deposit such duties and taxes, he shall pay to the district director of customs as liquidated damages an amount equal to the value of the merchandise plus the duties and taxes thereon (it being understood and agreed that the amount to be collected shall be based upon the quantity and value of such merchandise as determined by the district director of customs, and that the decision of the district director as to the status of such merchandise, whether free or dutiable, together with the rate and amount of duties and taxes, also shall be binding on all parties to this obligation);

(3) And if the above-bounden principal, when the merchandise is to be examined elsewhere than at the public stores, wharf, or other place in charge of a customs officer, shall hold such merchandise at the place to which it will be removed for examination until the merchandise shall have been released from the customs custody by the completion of final examination for purposes of appraisement; and, at any time before such release, shall transfer the merchandise to such place as the district director of customs may direct; and, when the merchandise has been corded and sealed, shall keep such cords and seals intact until removed by customs officers; or, in the event of default, shall pay to the district director of customs an amount equal to the value of the merchandise with respect to which there has been a default (as set forth in the entries therefor), plus the estimated duties and taxes thereon, as determined at the time of entry;

(4) And if in any case the above-bounden principal shall redeliver or cause to be redelivered to the order of the district director of customs, on demand by him, in accordance with the law and regulations in effect on the date of the release of said articles, any and all merchandise found not to comply with the law and regulations governing its admission into the commerce of the United States, unless before such demand the said principal shall have filed with the district director of customs a superseding bond on customs Form 7601 in which the actual owner whose declaration has been filed pursuant to section 485 (d), Tariff Act of 1930, shall have undertaken upon proper demand on such owner to effect such redelivery; or, in default of redelivery after a proper demand on him, the above-bounden principal shall pay to the said district director such amounts as liquidated damages as may be demanded by him in accordance with the law and regulations, not exceeding the amount of this obligation, for any breach or breaches thereof;

(5) And if in any case the above-bounden principal, in respect of any of the merchandise released from customs custody, shall redeliver or cause to be redelivered to the order of the district director of customs such additional packages or quantities of merchandise as may be desired by the appraiser pursuant to section 499, Tariff Act of 1930, as amended, for the purpose of examination, inspection, or appraisement, upon a demand made at any time before the appraiser's report of appraisement, unless before that time the said principal shall have filed with the district director of customs a superseding bond on customs Form 7601 in which the actual owner whose declaration has been filed pursuant to section 485 (d), Tariff Act of 1930, shall have undertaken upon proper demand on such owner to effect redelivery for such purposes; or, in default of redelivery after a proper demand on him, the above-bounden principal shall pay to the said district director such amounts as liquidated damages as may be demanded by him in accordance with the law and regulations, not exceeding the amount of this obligation, for any breach or breaches thereof;

(6) And if in any case the above-bounden principal shall redeliver or cause to be redelivered to the order of the district director of customs for marking pursuant to schedule 7, part 2, subpart E, headnote 4, Tariff Schedules of the United States, or section 304, Tariff Act of 1930, as amended, upon a demand made not later than twenty (20) days after the appraiser's report of appraisement, such of the merchandise as may have been released from customs custody, unless before that time the said principal shall have filed with the district director of customs a bond on customs Form 7601 in which the actual owner whose declaration has been filed pursuant to said section 485 (d) shall have undertaken upon proper demand on such owner to effect redelivery for such purposes; or, in default of redelivery after a proper demand on him, the above-bounden principal shall pay to the said district director such amounts as liquidated damages as may be demanded by him in accordance with the law and regulations, not exceeding the amount of this obligation, for any breach or breaches thereof;

(7) And if in the case of any and all merchandise found not to comply with the law and regulations governing its admission into the commerce of the United States, the above-bounden principal after proper notice shall mark, label, clean, fumigate, destroy, export, and do any and all other things in relation to said merchandise that may be lawfully required, and shall hold the said merchandise for inspection and examination, unless the said principal shall have filed with the district director of customs a bond on customs Form 7601 in which the actual owner whose declaration has been filed pursuant to section 485 (d) shall have undertaken after proper notice to mark, label, clean, fumigate, destroy, export, and do any and all other things in relation to the said merchandise that may be lawfully required, and to hold the said merchandise for inspection and examination; or in default thereof, shall pay to the district director of customs as liquidated damages an amount equal to the value of the merchandise with respect to which there has been a default, as set forth in the entry, plus the estimated duties thereon, as determined at the time of entry;

(8) And if in any case the above-bounden principal shall deliver to the district director of customs such invoices, declarations of owners or consignees, certificates of origin, certificates of exportation, and other documents as may be required by law or regulations in connection with the entry of said articles, and in the form and within the time required by law or regulations, or any lawful extension thereof, or in the event of failure to comply with any or all of the conditions of this section (8) shall pay to said district director such amounts as liquidated damages as may be demanded by him in accordance with the law and regulations, not exceeding the amount of this obligation, for any breach or breaches thereof;

Then this obligation shall be void; otherwise it shall remain in full force and effect.

Signed, sealed, and delivered in the presence of—

<table>
<tr><td>_Theresa Timanich, San Francisco, Ca._
(Name)</td><td>(Address)</td><td></td></tr>
<tr><td>_Rosalie L. McLan_, San Francisco, Ca.
(Name)</td><td>(Address)</td><td>_A. Lawrence Smith_ (SEAL)
(Principal)
A. Lawrence Smith jr.</td></tr>
<tr><td>________________
(Name)</td><td>________________
(Address)</td><td></td></tr>
<tr><td>________________
(Name)</td><td>________________
(Address)</td><td>THE ________ INSURANCE COMPANY (SEAL)
(Surety)</td></tr>
<tr><td>________________
(Name)</td><td>________________
(Address)</td><td></td></tr>
<tr><td>________________
(Name)</td><td>________________
(Address)</td><td>_David W. Sing_ (SEAL)
(Surety)
David W. SING
Attorney-in-Fact</td></tr>
</table>

CERTIFICATE AS TO CORPORATE PRINCIPAL

I,____, certify that I am the* ________________________ of the

corporation named as principal in the within bond; that ____, who signed

the said bond on behalf of the principal, was then ________________________________ of said corporation; that I know his

signature, and his signature thereto is genuine; and that said bond was duly signed, sealed, and attested for and in behalf of

said corporation by authority of its governing body.

____ [Corporate Seal]

(To be used when no power of attorney has been filed with the district director of customs)

**May be executed by the secretary, assistant secretary, or other officer of the corporation.*

Ports of entry by state
(Including Puerto Rico and the US Virgin Islands)

ALABAMA
Birmingham
Huntsville
Mobile**

ALASKA
Alcan
Anchorage**
Dalton Cache
Fairbanks
Juneau
Ketchikan
Sitka
Skagway
Valdez
Wrangell

ARIZONA
Douglas
Lukeville
Naco
Nogales**
Phoenix
San Luis
Sasabe

ARKANSAS
Little Rock
N. Little Rock

CALIFORNIA
Andrade
Calexico
Eureka
Fresno
Los Angeles°
Long Beach°
Port San Luis
San Diego**
San Francisco**
Oakland**
Tecate
San Ysidro

COLORADO
Denver

CONNECTICUT
Bridgeport**
Hartford
New Haven
New London

DELAWARE
Wilmington

DISTRICT OF COLUMBIA
Washington**

FLORIDA
Apalachicola
Boca Grande
Carrabelle
Fernandina Beach
Jacksonville
Key West
Miami°
Orlando
Panama City
Pensacola
Port Canaveral
Port Everglades
Port St. Joe
St. Petersburg
Tampa**
West Palm Beach

GEORGIA
Atlanta
Brunswick
Savannah**

HAWAII
Honolulu**
Hilo
Kahului
Nawiliwili
Port Allen

IDAHO
Eastport
Porthill

ILLINOIS
Chicago°
Peoria

INDIANA
Evansville
Indianapolis
Lawrenceburg

IOWA
Des Moines

KANSAS
Wichita

KENTUCKY
Louisville
Owensboro

LOUISIANA
Baton Rouge
Gramercy
Lake Charles
Morgan City
New Orleans°

MAINE
Bangor
Bar Harbor
Bath
Belfast
Bridgewater
Calais
Eastport
Fort Fairfield
Fort Kent
Houlton
Jackman
Jonesport
Limestone
Madawaska
Portland**
Rockland
Van Buren
Vanceboro

MARYLAND
Annapolis
Baltimore**
Cambridge

MASSACHUSETTS
Boston°
Fall River
Gloucester
Lawrence
New Bedford
Plymouth
Salem
Springfield
Worcester

MICHIGAN
Battle Creek
Detroit
Grand Rapids
Muskegon
Port Huron
Saginaw
Bay City/Flint
Sault Ste. Marie

MINNESOTA
Baudette
Duluth**
Superior, Wis.
Grand Portage
International Falls
Minneapolis**
St. Paul
Noyes
Pinecreek
Roseau
Warroad

MISSISSIPPI
Greenville
Gulfport
Pascagoula
Vicksburg

MISSOURI
Kansas City
St. Joseph
St. Louis**
Springfield

MONTANA
Butte
Del Bonita
Great Falls**
Morgan
Opheim
Piegan
Raymond
Roosville
Scobey
Sweetgrass
Turner
Whitetail
Whitlash

NEBRASKA
Omaha

NEVADA
Las Vegas
Reno

NEW HAMPSHIRE
Portsmouth

NEW JERSEY
Perth Amboy

NEW MEXICO
Albuquerque
Columbus

NEW YORK
Albany
Alexandria Bay
Buffalo**
Niagara Falls
Cape Vincent
Champlain
Rouses Point
Chateaugay
Clayton
Fort Covington
Messena
New York
  Kennedy Airpt.
  Newark
  NY Seaport
Ogdensburg
Oswego
Rochester
Sodus Point
Syracuse
Trout River
Utica

NORTH CAROLINA
Beaufort-Morehead City
Charlotte
Durham
Reidsville
Wilmington**
Winston-Salem

NORTH DAKOTA
Ambrose
Antler
Carbury
Dunseith
Fortuna
Hannah
Hansboro

Maida
Neche
Noonan
Northgate
Pembina**
Portal
Sarles
Sherwood
St. John
Walhalla
Westhope

OHIO
Akron
Ashtabula/Conneaut
Cincinnati
Cleveland**
Columbus
Dayton
Sundusky
Toledo

OKLAHOMA
Oklahoma City
Tulsa

OREGON
Coos Bay
Newport
Portland**†

PENNSYLVANIA
Chester
Erie
Harrisburg
Philadelphia**
Pittsburgh
Wilkes-Barre
Scranton

PUERTO RICO
Aguadilla
Fajardo
Guanica
Humacao
Jobos
Mayaguez
Ponce
San Juan**

RHODE ISLAND
Newport
Providence**

SOUTH CAROLINA
Charleston
Georgetown
Greenville
Spartanburg

TENNESSEE
Chattanooga
Knoxville
Memphis
Nashville

TEXAS
Amarillo
Austin
Beaumont†
Brownsville
Corpus Christi
Dallas**
Ft. Worth
Del Rio
Eagle Pass
El Paso
Fabens
Freeport
Hidalgo
Houston°
Galveston
Laredo**
Lubbock
Orange†
Port Authur**†
Port Lavaca
Point Comfort
Presidio
Progresso
Rio Grande City
Roma
Sabine†
San Antonio

UTAH
Salt Lake City

VERMONT
Beecher Falls
Burlington
Derby Line
Highgate Springs
Alburg
Norton
Richford
St. Albans**

VIRGIN ISLANDS
Charlotte Amalie**
St. Thomas
Christiansted
Coral Bay
Cruz Bay
Frederiksted

VIRGINIA
Alexandria
Cape Charles City
Norfolk-Newport News**
Reedville
Richmond-Petersburg

WASHINGTON
Aberdeen
Anacortes†
Bellingham†
Blaine
Boundary
Danville
Everett†
Ferry
Friday Harbor†
Frontier
Laurier
Longview†
Lynden
Metaline Falls
Neah Bay†
Nighthawk
Olympia†
Oroville
Point Roberts
Port Angeles†
Port Townsend†
Seattle**†
Spokane
Sumas
Tacoma†

WEST VIRGINIA
Charleston**

WISCONSIN
Ashland
Green Bay
Manitowoc
Marinette
Milwaukee**
Racine
Sheboygan

†Consolidated Ports
°Regional Headquarters
**Districts

Customs regions and districts

Headquarters
U.S. Customs Service
1301 Constitution Ave., N.W.
Washington, D.C. 20229

Northeast Region
Boston, MA 02110

Districts:
Portland, ME 04111
St. Albans, VT 05478
Boston, MA 02109
Providence, R.I. 02903
Buffalo, NY 14202
Ogdensburg, NY 13669
Bridgeport, CT 06609
Philadelphia, PA 19106
Baltimore, MD 21202
Norfolk, VA 23510
Washington, D.C. 20041

New York Region
New York, NY 10048

Districts:
New York Seaport Area
New York, NY 10048
Kennedy Airport Area
Jamaica, NY 11430
Newark Area
Newark, NJ 07114

Southeast Region
Miami, FL 33131

Districts:
Wilmington, N.C. 28401
San Juan, P.R. 00903
Charleston, S.C. 29402
Savannah, GA 31401
Tampa, FL 33601
Miami, FL 33131
St. Thomas, V.I. 00801

South Central Region
New Orleans, LA 70130

Districts:
Mobil, AL 36602
New Orleans, LA 70130

Southwest Region
Houston, TX 77002

Districts:
Port Arthur, TX 77640
Galveston, TX 77550
Houston, TX 77052
Laredo, TX 78040
El Paso, TX 79985
Dallas
Ft. Worth, TX 75261

Pacific Region
Los Angeles, CA 90053

Districts:
Nogales, AZ 85621
San Diego, CA 92188
Los Angeles, CA
San Pedro, CA 90731
San Francisco, CA 94126
Honolulu, HI 96806
Portland, OR 97209
Seattle, WA 98174
Anchorage, AK 99501
Great Falls, MT 59401

North Central Region
Chicago, IL 60603

Districts:
Chicago, IL 60607
Pembina, ND 58271
Minneapolis
St. Paul, MN 55401
Duluth, MN 55802
Milwaukee, WI 53202
Cleveland, OH 44114
St. Louis, MO 63105
Detroit, MI 48226

US customs officers in foreign countries

Customs Attache
U.S. Mission to the European
   Communities (USEC)
No. 40 Blvd. du Regent
1000 Brussels, Belgium

Customs Attache
American Embassy
100 Wellington St.
Ottawa, Ontario K1P5T2 Canada

Customs Attache
American Embassy
24/31 Grosvenor Square
London, W. 1 England

Customs Attache
American Embassy
58 Rue la Boetie, Rm 210
75008 Paris, France

Senior Customs Repre.
American Consulate General
57th Floor, Hopewell Bldg.
Queen's Road East, Wanchai
Hong Kong

Customs Attache
American Embassy
Via V. Vento 119
Rome, Italy

Customs Attache
American Embassy
10-5, 1-chrome Akasaka
Minato-ku, Tokyo 107 Japan

Customs Attache
American Embassy
Paseo de la Reforma 305
Colonia Cuahtemoc
Mexico, D. F. Mexico

Customs Attache
American Embassy
Mehlemer Ave 5300
Bonn-Bad Godesberg, West
   Germany

Chapter 5

EPA requirements

Requirements

Reproduced on the following pages is the Automotive Imports-Fact Sheet published by the EPA. This document gives summarized requirements that have to be met when importing a car.

Form Approved
OMB No. 2000-0228
Exp. 05/31/85

AUTOMOTIVE IMPORTS - FACT SHEET

WARNING: Except for driving a nonconforming vehicle imported under bond from the port of entry to the vehicle owner's residence or to the location where modification/testing work is to be performed, it is a violation of the Clean Air Act to operate such a vehicle on public streets or highways or to sell it prior to final release by the U. S. Customs Service.

The Clean Air Act requires that every motor vehicle imported into the United States comply with the emission requirements that are applicable to the model year in which the vehicle was manufactured. <u>Emission requirements are applicable to 1968 and later model year gasoline-fueled vehicles and 1975 and later model year diesel-fueled vehicles.</u> It should be noted that a manufacturer's model year usually begins during the late summer or early autumn of the previous calendar year. For example, a vehicle manufactured in July 1977 would be a 1978 model. Also, <u>motorcycles manufactured after December 31, 1977, and gasoline-fueled and diesel-fueled engines manufactured after January 1, 1970, for use in heavy-duty vehicles,</u> must meet Federal emission requirements.

1971 and later model year vehicles manufactured in conformity with Federal emission requirements may be identified by a label installed by the manufacturer in the engine compartment. The label will be entitled "Vehicle Emission Control Information" and will contain the name and trademark of the manufacturer. Conforming motorcycles will have a similar label located on their frame. Conforming 1968 through 1970 vehicles will not have an EPA label, but they may be identified by the presence of a label on the vehicle's doorpost specifying conformity with Federal motor vehicle safety standards. <u>A vehicle which does not have a label almost certainly does not conform with U. S. emission requirements.</u>

The Clean Air Act permits conditional importation of a nonconforming vehicle, provided that a bond, equal to the value of the vehicle, plus duty, is posted with the U. S. Customs Service. The importer then has 90 days to bring the vehicle into conformity. Nonconforming vehicles which are imported must either be modified to make them identical to those certified for sale in the United States, or tested to demonstrate compliance with U. S. air pollution standards. Otherwise, such vehicles must be exported or destroyed.

One Time Exemption

There are very limited exceptions to these importation requirements. An individual who has never before imported a nonconforming vehicle may do so, one-time-only, for personal use and not for resale, if the vehicle is at least <u>five model years old</u> at the time of importation, without bringing it into conformity with U. S. emission requirements. (For the purpose of this policy, model year age is determined from January 1 of the calendar year; i. e., as of January 1, 1983, 1978 and older model year vehicles would qualify.) See first paragraph on first page for definition of model year. Also, an individual who is permanently immigrating to the U. S. may import one nonconforming vehicle of any model year, for personal use and not for resale, at the time of immigration. Vehicles imported under these procedures must still be bonded at the time of entry and must be modified to meet U. S. safety requirements (see page FS-5) PLUS ANY STATE OR LOCAL EMISSION REQUIREMENTS. If you import such a vehicle, you must fill out the forms Customs will give you at the port of entry, post the bond and pay the import duty. Customs will send us the EPA form (EPA Form 3520-1) and we will issue a release on the vehicle within 90 days. You do not have to apply for the five model year exemption; it will be granted automatically after importation. It cannot be granted before you import your vehicle. You must apply in writing, to the address on page FS-5, for the immigrant exemption and provide proof of immigrant status. After you have completed the safety modifications on the vehicle and receive a release from the Department of Transportation (DOT), the bond will be refunded to you. A vehicle imported under these procedures must be owned by the individual importer before importation and cannot be resold in the U. S. for at least two years after importation unless it is first brought into conformity with U. S. emission requirements. This exemption does not apply to importations by a commercial enterprise or business agent or to importations arranged by persons for other individuals. THESE EXEMPTIONS ARE NOT VALID IN CALIFORNIA.

Modification Option

Modification of a nonconforming vehicle consists of replacing, adding, or deleting components to make the vehicle identical to a version certified for sale in the U. S. In order to modify a nonconforming vehicle, you must first obtain written modification instructions from the manufacturer's U. S. representative. (See enclosed list.)

Since this Agency certifies only those vehicles which are intended for sale in the United States, we cannot provide information on the modifications necessary to bring foreign models into conformity with United States emission requirements. Modifications based on instructions from any source other than the U. S. representative of the manufacturer are not acceptable. Likewise, modifications derived from service manuals or statements from dealers or service facilities located overseas that a vehicle was manufactured in conformity, or has been modified to bring it into conformity, are not acceptable.

Modification of a nonconforming vehicle is usually not possible. Many vehicles available overseas were never certified by their manufacturers for sale in the United

States. Hence, there is no certified version with which to demonstrate conformity. Further, most manufacturer's representatives will not provide modification instructions to an importer and this Agency cannot require them to do so; testing your vehicle via the Federal Test Procedure is then the only option available to demonstrate conformity.

Testing Option

Testing a vehicle to demonstrate compliance with U. S. air pollution standards consists of having the vehicle tested at a qualified laboratory (see enclosed list) according to the Federal Test Procedure (FTP). The cost of such a test is high ($850 or more) and the risk of failing it is also high for vehicles not originally manufactured to meet U. S. standards. <u>Evidence that a vehicle has passed an emission inspection test administered by a state (including California), or a test conducted at a dealership, does not demonstrate conformity with Federal emission requirements.</u> The FTP is a comprehensive test involving a prescribed sequence of cold starting, hot starting and vehicle operating conditions, performed on a chassis dynamometer. It determines hydrocarbon, carbon monoxide, oxides of nitrogen, evaporative and, where applicable, diesel particulate emissions from a vehicle while it is actually being driven. A state test measures only the hydrocarbon and carbon monoxide emissions from a vehicle during a very short test.

If you elect to have a vehicle tested to demonstrate compliance with U. S. air pollution standards, a qualified testing laboratory must provide this Agency with evidence that the vehicle was tested in accordance with the proper procedures. The evidence includes a notarized copy of an EPA test report form (copy enclosed) listing all the modifications performed on the vehicle to enable it to pass the test, the complete test results and accompanied by clear photographs of the modifications. <u>Note that if the vehicle is modified by installation of a catalytic converter it must also be equipped with a fuel filler restrictor and "unleaded fuel only" labels to insure the use of unleaded gasoline.</u> The test laboratory will send the completed test packet to EPA. After we receive the test packet, we will review it and, if the vehicle was successfully tested, send a release letter to Customs and a copy to the importer.

Catalytic Converter Replacement

If you are reimporting a U. S. version vehicle, with EPA and DOT labels affixed and equipped with a catalytic converter, which has been driven outside North America (i. e., outside the United States, Canada or Mexico) the catalytic converter will have been deactivated because only leaded gasoline is available in such areas. Lead in gasoline poisons the catalytic material. Therefore, when the vehicle is reimported into the U. S., you will have to post a bond with Customs, fill out an EPA Form 3520-1 (which will be provided by Customs at the time of importation) and the catalytic converter will have to be replaced. Also, if your vehicle is a 1981 or newer model and is equipped with an oxygen sensor, the sensor will have to be cleaned or replaced, per the vehicle manufacturer's instructions. The vehicle's fuel filler restrictor will have to be replaced if it has been removed or disabled.

In order to secure the release of your bond, <u>have the catalytic converter replaced with a new converter</u> (on some vehicles only the catalytic material need be replaced, rather than the entire converter - check with the vehicle manufacturer) have the oxygen sensor cleaned or replaced and have the filler restrictor replaced, if necessary. Submit a clear copy of the work order from the facility where the work was done stating that: the catalyst has been replaced; the oxygen sensor has been cleaned or replaced or the vehicle is not equipped with a sensor; and, the fuel filler restrictor has been replaced or inspected and is intact. Include your name, address and the vehicle identification number (VIN) on the work order, a copy of the EPA Form 3520-1 and send this to EPA at the address on page FS-5.

If you are contemplating exporting your U. S. version vehicle outside of North America, you may obtain a waiver to have the catalytic converter removed before export so that upon return of the vehicle to the U. S. it will only have to be reinstalled, rather than replaced. For information concerning a waiver, call 202-382-2637.

<u>Release of Bond - Time Extension</u>

Final admission of a vehicle and release of the bond cannot be made until we receive the required information. If you do not take appropriate action within 90 days from the entry date of your vehicle, we will assume that you do not intend to demonstrate conformity, and will ask Customs to request redelivery of the vehicle.

In the event that you are unable to complete the modifications or test the vehicle within the 90 day time limit, an extension of time on the bond may be requested in writing from the Customs office (not from EPA) where the vehicle was imported. Justification for the extension must be provided to Customs.

If you are unable to demonstrate conformity because of expense or any other reason, your vehicle must be exported redelivered to Customs or destroyed. Failure to dispose of the vehicle by one of these methods will subject you to assessment of liquidated damages by Customs up to the amount of the bond and a fine of up to $10,000 und Clean Air Act.

NOTE: As stated above, modification of a nonconforming vehicle is usually not possible. Also, testing can be an expensive and frustrating experience, since the nearest test laboratory may be hundreds of miles from your home and the modifications that are necessary for your vehicle to pass the test may be extensive. Even if you are successful in demonstrating conformity of your vehicle, you may experience additional problems. Because your vehicle contains foreign-version components, parts and service may be difficult to obtain and the vehicle may not be covered by any warranty. <u>Also, your state may have additional restrictions on the registration of a vehicle imported under these provisions.</u> Check with your state Division of Motor Vehicles.

BECAUSE OF THE EXPENSE, INCONVENIENCE AND POTENTIAL ASSESSMENTS AND FINES INVOLVED WITH IMPORTING AN UNCERTIFIED VEHICLE AND MAKING THAT VEHICLE MEET FEDERAL EMISSION (AND SAFETY - SEE BELOW) REQUIREMENTS, WE STRONGLY RECOMMEND THAT YOU ONLY PURCHASE A VEHICLE CERTIFIED AND LABELED BY THE MANUFACTURER FOR SALE IN THE U. S.

Additional Information

If you have any questions that are not answered by this fact sheet, you may contact the Investigation/Imports Section by telephone at <u>202-382-2504</u>, or by mail at:

> Investigation/Imports Section
> MOD (EN-340F)
> U. S. EPA
> Washington, DC 20460

When calling EPA, please have available the make, model, year and vehicle identification number (VIN) of your vehicle (from the registration card) and, if it has already been imported, the port of entry, date of entry and entry number (from the EPA Form 3520-1). When writing to EPA, include this information, plus a telephone number (with area code) where you can be reached during the day.

Federal safety standards are the responsibility of the U. S. Department of Transportation, rather than the Environmental Protection Agency. Therefore, questions concerning safety requirements should be directed to the following individual for response:

> Director, Office of Vehicle Safety Compliance
> National Highway Traffic Safety Administration
> U. S. Department of Transportation
> Washington, DC 20590
> 202-426-1693

Enclosures

Rev. 6/83

MOTOR VEHICLE EMISSION TEST REPORT FORM

Form Approved
OMB No. 2000-0228
Exp. 05/31/85

> WARNING: Any person who knowingly makes a false statement on this form is in violation of Federal law and may be fined not more than $10,000 or imprisoned not more than five years, or both. 18 USC 1001.

The Following Items Are To Be Filled In By Importer (Or Consignee) From EPA Form 3520-1

Name and Address of Importer (Or Consignee)	
	Port of Entry
	Date of Entry
	Customs Entry No.

The Following Items Are To Be Filled In By Test Laboratory

Name of Test Laboratory	Address of Test Laboratory	Date of Test	
Make of Vehicle	Model of Vehicle	Model Year of Vehicle	Mileage at Time of Test
Vehicle or Chassis Identification No.		Engine Serial No.	Vehicle Curb Weight
Test Procedure		Inertia Weight Class	Transmission Type Auto/Manual
Equipped with PCV System Yes/No	Equipped with Air Conditioning Yes/No	Equipped with Fuel Filler Neck Restrictor Yes/No	"Unleaded Fuel Only" Labels Installed Yes/No
Description of Emission Control Modifications		Photographs of Modifications Enclosed Yes/No	Modifications Performed by:

TEST RESULTS		ALTERNATIVE STANDARDS (See Chart on Back)
HC =	GPM	
CO =	GPM	
NOx =	GPM	
Evap =	GPT	
Part =	GPM	

GPM = Grams per Mile

GPT = Grams per Test

I CERTIFY THAT THE ABOVE VEHICLE HAS BEEN TESTED IN ACCORDANCE WITH TEST PROCEDURES OUTLINED IN 40 CFR 85.075-9 THROUGH 28 (FOR 1968 THROUGH 1977 MODELS) OR 40 CFR, PART 86 (FOR 1978 AND LATER MODELS) AND THAT THE ITEMS FILLED IN BY THE TEST LABORATORY AND THE OFFICIAL FEDERAL TEST PROCEDURE RESULTS SHOWN ABOVE ARE CORRECT.

____
Signature of Corporate Officer

Subscribed and Sworn To Before Me
This______________Day of__________________, 19_____

Notary Public
My Commission Expires:__________________________

Rev. 8/82 - Previous edition obsolete

Federal Emission Standards for Light-Duty Vehicles
(Expressed as grams per mile (gpm) and grams per test (gpt))

1970 - 1984 Model Year Vehicles

	1970	1971	1972	1973-1974	1975-1976	1977	1978-1979	1980	1981-1984
HC	4.1 gpm	4.1 gpm	3.0 gpm	3.0 gpm	1.5 gpm	1.5 gpm	1.5 gpm	.41 gpm	.41 gpm
CO	34 gpm	34 gpm	28 gpm	28 gpm	15 gpm	15 gpm	15 gpm	7.0 gpm	3.4 gpm
NOx	N. R.	N. R.	N. R.	3.1 gpm	3.1 gpm	2.0 gpm	2.0 gpm	2.0 gpm	1.0 gpm
Evap.*	N. R.	6 gpt	2 gpt	2 gpt	2 gpt	2 gpt	6.0 gpt (SHED)**	6.0 gpt (SHED)**	2.0 gpt (SHED)**
Diesel Particulates									0.60 gpm*** (82 and later)

HC = Hydrocarbons   NOx = Oxides of Nitrogen   N. R. = Not Required
CO = Carbon Monoxide   Evap.= Evaporative Hydrocarbons

1968 - 1969 Model Year Vehicles

For information on emission standards applicable to 1968 - 1969 model year vehicles, call EPA at 202-382-2504.

All 1968 and later model year gasoline-fueled vehicles must be equipped with a closed crankcase system.
*   Evaporative emission testing is not required on diesel-fueled vehicles.
**   Evaporative emission testing for 1978 and later model year vehicles must be done according to the SHED procedure.
*** Particulate standard applies only to 1982 and later model year diesel-fueled vehicles.

Rev. 1/84

Customs form

The following form is completed at time of submission of import to US customs. It (OMB No. 2000-0041) is sent by US customs to EPA informing the agency of your importation of an auto.

Form Approved
OMB No. 2000-0041

<table>
<tr><td colspan="2">U.S. ENVIRONMENTAL PROTECTION AGENCY</td><td rowspan="2">WARNING
Any person who knowingly makes a false declaration shall be fined not more than $10,000 or imprisoned not more than 5 years, or both. 18 U.S.C. 1001.</td></tr>
<tr><td colspan="2">IMPORTATION OF MOTOR VEHICLES AND MOTOR VEHICLE ENGINES SUBJECT TO FEDERAL AIR POLLUTION CONTROL REGULATIONS
(Read instructions on reverse side before completing form.)</td></tr>
</table>

PORT OF ENTRY	DATE OF ENTRY	ENTRY NO. (If applicable)

IMPORT VESSEL OR CARRIER	MAKE OF VEHICLE (or engine, if not chassis mounted or if mounted in heavy-duty vehicle)	MODEL OF VEHICLE (or engine, if not chassis mounted or if mounted in heavy-duty vehicle)

MODEL YEAR OF VEHICLE (or engine, if not chassis mounted or if mounted in heavy-duty vehicle)	VEHICLE IDENTIFICATION NUMBER	ENGINE SERIAL NUMBER (If not chassis mounted or if mounted in heavy-duty vehicle)

✓ WITH REGARD TO THE IMPORTATION OF THE DESCRIBED MOTOR VEHICLE OR MOTOR VEHICLE ENGINE, I DECLARE THAT:

1. SUCH 1971 OR SUBSEQUENT MODEL YEAR MOTOR VEHICLE OR MOTOR VEHICLE ENGINE IS COVERED BY A CERTIFICATE OF CONFORMITY ISSUED BY THE DEPARTMENT OF HEALTH, EDUCATION, AND WELFARE OR BY THE U.S. ENVIRONMENTAL PROTECTION AGENCY, AND BEARS A CERTIFICATION LABEL OR TAG.

2. SUCH 1968, 1969 OR 1970 MODEL YEAR MOTOR VEHICLE OR MOTOR VEHICLE ENGINE IS COVERED BY A CERTIFICATE OF CONFORMITY ISSUED BY THE DEPARTMENT OF HEALTH, EDUCATION, AND WELFARE OR THE U.S. ENVIRONMENTAL PROTECTION AGENCY.

WITH REGARD TO THE IMPORTATION OF THE DESCRIBED MOTOR VEHICLE OR ENGINE, I DECLARE THAT SUCH VEHICLE OR ENGINE IS NOT COVERED BY A CERTIFICATE OF CONFORMITY ISSUED BY THE DEPARTMENT OF HEALTH, EDUCATION, AND WELFARE OR THE U.S. ENVIRONMENTAL PROTECTION AGENCY, BUT IS ELIGIBLE FOR ADMISSION INTO THE UNITED STATES BECAUSE:

3. THE VEHICLE OR ENGINE IS BEING IMPORTED SOLELY FOR PURPOSES OF DISPLAY AND WILL NOT BE SOLD OR OPERATED ON THE PUBLIC HIGHWAYS.

4. THE IMPORTER OR CONSIGNEE IS A MEMBER OF THE ARMED FORCES OF A FOREIGN COUNTRY, OR MEMBER OF THE SECRETARIAT OF A PUBLIC INTERNATIONAL ORGANIZATION SO DESIGNATED PURSUANT TO 60 STAT. 669 (22 U.S.C. 288(b)) OR A MEMBER OF THE PERSONNEL OF A FOREIGN GOVERNMENT ON ASSIGNMENT IN THE UNITED STATES WHO COMES WITHIN THE CLASS OF PERSONS FOR WHOM FREE ENTRY OF VEHICLES HAS BEEN AUTHORIZED BY THE DEPARTMENT OF STATE AND THE VEHICLE OR ENGINE WILL NOT BE SOLD IN THE UNITED STATES.

5. THE IMPORTER OR CONSIGNEE IS A NON-RESIDENT OF THE UNITED STATES IMPORTING SUCH VEHICLE OR ENGINE FOR PERSONAL USE FOR NOT MORE THAN ONE YEAR FROM THE DATE OF ENTRY, AND THE VEHICLE OR ENGINE WILL NOT BE SOLD IN THE UNITED STATES.

6. THE VEHICLE OR ENGINE IS BEING IMPORTED FOR THE PURPOSE OF TESTING AND WILL NOT BE SOLD OR OPERATED ON THE PUBLIC HIGHWAYS WITHOUT THE PRIOR WRITTEN CONSENT OF THE ADMINISTRATOR OF THE U.S. ENVIRONMENTAL PROTECTION AGENCY.

7. THE VEHICLE OR ENGINE IS INTENDED SOLELY FOR EXPORT.

8. THE VEHICLE OR ENGINE IS NOT SUBJECT TO THE REGULATIONS UNDER THE CLEAN AIR ACT BECAUSE IT IS A:

   a. VEHICLE MANUFACTURED BEFORE THE 1968 MODEL YEAR.

   b. NON-CHASSIS MOUNTED ENGINE TO BE USED IN A LIGHT-DUTY VEHICLE.
   (NOTE: A light-duty vehicle is a vehicle designed primarily for transportation of property and rated at 6,000 pounds GVW or less or designed primarily for transportation of persons with a capacity of 12 persons or less.)

   c. ENGINE MANUFACTURED BEFORE JANUARY 1, 1970 FOR USE IN A HEAVY-DUTY VEHICLE.
   (NOTE: A heavy-duty vehicle is a vehicle designed primarily for transportation of property and rated at more than 6,000 pounds GVW or designed primarily for transportation of persons with a capacity of more than 12 persons.)

   d. LIGHT-DUTY NON-GASOLINE FUELED VEHICLE. *(If diesel-fueled, only for 1974 and earlier models)*

   e. MOTORCYCLE MANUFACTURED BEFORE JANUARY 1, 1978

   f. RACING VEHICLE NOT TO BE OPERATED ON PUBLIC STREETS OR HIGHWAYS.

9. THE VEHICLE OR ENGINE IS ONE OF A CLASS OF VEHICLES OR ENGINES FOR WHICH AN APPLICATION FOR A CERTIFICATE OF CONFORMITY IS PENDING BEFORE THE ADMINISTRATOR OF THE U.S. ENVIRONMENTAL PROTECTION AGENCY, AND IS BEING IMPORTED UNDER BOND.

10. THE VEHICLE OR ENGINE IS NOT IN CONFORMITY WITH APPLICABLE EMISSION STANDARDS, BUT WILL BE BROUGHT INTO CONFORMITY WITH SUCH STANDARDS, AND IS BEING IMPORTED UNDER BOND.

11. NEITHER THE IMPORTER NOR THE ULTIMATE CONSIGNEE POSSESSES SUFFICIENT INFORMATION TO MAKE ANY OF THE PRECEDING DECLARATIONS, BUT THE IMPORTER OR ULTIMATE CONSIGNEE WILL SEEK TO DETERMINE SUCH INFORMATION, AND THE VEHICLE OR ENGINE IS BEING IMPORTED UNDER BOND.

WARNING: Entry under provisions 9, 10, and 11 requires posting of bond at the time of entry equal to the value of the merchandise plus duty for delivery of a conformity statement no later than 90 days after entry to the District Director of Customs. Written notice that a vehicle or engine has been admitted under bond must be sent by the importer not later than 5 days after entry to the U.S. Environmental Protection Agency, Manufacturers Operations Division (EN-340), Washington, D.C. 20460. The information required in such notice is set forth in the instructions printed below on this form. A vehicle admitted under bond must be redelivered to port of entry unless certification is granted, or the Administrator makes a determination in writing that the vehicle has been modified to conform to applicable standards.

NAME OF IMPORTER (Please print)	NAME OF CONSIGNEE (Please print)

ADDRESS OF IMPORTER	ADDRESS OF CONSIGNEE

SIGNATURE OF IMPORTER OR CONSIGNEE

EPA Form 3520-1 (Rev. 3-81)   EDITION OF 5-80 MAY BE USED.

INSTRUCTIONS

This form is used to determine whether a motor vehicle or motor vehicle engine can be imported into the United States.

This form must be filled out for all motor vehicles and motor vehicle engines which are imported into the United States. If there is more than one vehicle or engine in an entry, only one form needs to be filled out, provided the information on the make, model, model year and vehicle identification or engine serial numbers are provided for each vehicle or engine on an attached sheet.

SPECIAL INSTRUCTIONS FOR ITEMS 9, 10, and 11

Item

9   Admission Pending Certification. A vehicle or engine imported under a declaration that it is one of a class of vehicles or engines represented by test vehicles or engines for which an application for certification of conformity is pending before the U.S. Environmental Protection Agency may be conditionally admitted into the United States under bond, but will be denied final admission unless the importer or consignee follows these instructions:

1. The importer or consignee must submit to the Administrator within 5 days following conditional admission a written request that the vehicle be conditionally admitted pending certification. The written request must:

    a.   Identify the test vehicle or engine which represents the vehicle or engine offered for importation.

    b. Identify the place where the vehicle or engine will be stored while the application for certification is pending before the Administrator. (See storage requirement below)

    c.   Acknowledge responsibility for custody of the vehicle while certification is pending.

The certificate of conformity must be issued by the U.S. Environmental Protection Agency before the vehicle or engine may be granted final admission.

Reference: 40 C.F.R. §85.1503

10   Admission Pending Modification. A vehicle or engine imported under a declaration that it is not covered by a certificate of conformity, but that it will be brought into conformity with standards may be conditionally admitted into the United States under bond, but will be denied final admission unless the importer or consignee follows these instructions:

1. The importer or consignee must submit to the U.S. Environmental Protection Agency within 5 days following conditional admission a written request that he be permitted to modify the vehicle or engine so that it will be in conformity with applicable emission standards. The written request must:

    a.   Specify the modifications necessary to bring the vehicle or engine into conformity with a test vehicle or engine for which a certificate of conformity has been granted. (NOTE: It is the importer's responsibility to determine from the manufacturer of the vehicle or engine to be imported what modifications are necessary.)

    b.   Specify the date by which the necessary modifications will be made.

    c.   Identify the place where the vehicle or engine will be stored until the U.S. Environmental Protection Agency determines that it has been brought into conformity with emission standards. (See storage requirements below.)

    d.   Acknowledge responsibility for custody of the vehicle or engine while the modifications are being made and a determination of conformity is pending.

    e.   Authorize representatives of the U.S. Environmental Protection Agency to inspect or test the vehicle or engine at any reasonable time in order to make a determination of conformity.

2. The importer or consignee must obtain the written determination of the U.S. Environmental Protection Agency that the vehicle or engine has been modified to conform to standards.

3. If the vehicle or engine cannot be modified to bring it within a class of vehicles or engines represented by a test vehicle or engine for which a certificate of conformity has been issued, the importer or consignee must undertake to demonstrate that the vehicle or engine is in conformity with emission standards by having the vehicle tested in accordance with the regulations of the U.S. Environmental Protection Agency.

Reference 40 C.F.R. §85.1504

11   Admission Pending Receipt of Information. A vehicle or engine imported under a declaration that the importer or consignee does not possess sufficient information to make a knowledgeable declaration may be conditionally admitted into the United States under bond, but will be denied final admission unless the importer or consignee follows these instructions:

1. The importer or consignee must submit to the U.S. Environmental Protection Agency a written request that the vehicle or engine be conditionally admitted pending receipt of information to determine whether the vehicle or engine is covered by a certificate of conformity, or what modifications, if any, are necessary to bring the vehicle into conformity with standards. The written request must:

    a.   Identify the place where the vehicle or engine will be stored pending receipt of information. (See storage requirement below.)

    b.   Acknowledge responsibility for custody of the vehicle or engine pending receipt of information.

2. The importer or consignee must redeclare the vehicle or engine under the item determined to be appropriate.

Reference: 40 C.F.R. §85.1505

STORAGE REQUIREMENT AND PROHIBITION OF OPERATION OR SALE OF VEHICLES CONDITIONALLY ADMITTED UNDER ITEMS 9, 10, and 11

A vehicle or engine conditionally admitted pending certification, modification, or receipt of information must be stored and may not be operated on the public highways or sold until the vehicle or engine is granted final admission and the bond is released.

A vehicle or engine conditionally admitted shall not be stored on the premises, or subject to access by or control of, any dealer. (NOTE: The importer or consignee may request that this prohibition be waived if modifications of a vehicle or engine to bring it into conformity must be performed by a dealer.)

Failure to comply with these instructions can subject the importer to a fine up to the amount of $10,000 per vehicle or engine.

Reference: 40 C.F.R. §85.205, 85.1508

Completed forms should be sent by the Bureau of Customs to: U.S. Environmental Protection Agency
Manufacturers Operations Division (EN-340)
Washington, D.C. 20460

EPA Form 3520-1 (Rev. 3-81) Reverse

Waiver

Every auto imported to the United States must meet emissions requirements as set by law and administered by the US Environmental Protection Agency (EPA). In addition, some states have their own requirements which are equal to or more stringent than those of the EPA (such as California). EPA waives its requirement if you import your auto under the one-time exemption. These rules apply: one, that you import under your Social Security number (entered on the forms for entry purposes); and two, that the auto be five years or older to qualify under this policy. An exemption is automatic (a matter of policy, not law, so could be changed), but you should write and request it. (A sample request letter is shown below.) All requests for exemption plus all correspondence to all US government entities should be sent via certified or registered mail.

(current date)

Director US Environmental Protection Agency
Manufacturer Operations Division
EN 340 Washington, DC 20460

Dear Sir:

On __(date)__ I imported a __(year and make of car)__ into the United States. This letter is to request a waiver from the EPA regulations for this car.

I imported the car under my Social Security number for my own personal use and not for resale. The serial number of the car is ___________________ . My Social Security number is ___________________ . Entry number of the car (US customs) is ___________________ . The port of entry was ___________________ . The engine number is ___________________ .

Please contact me if you need more information.

Sincerely,

(name, address, telephone)

Petition for Mitigation

In case you cannot bring the car into conformation with EPA requirements and have *not* taken advantage of the one-time waiver policy (if available), a Petition for Mitigation (OMB No. 2000-0228) can be submitted to EPA. Submission of the petition does not automatically mean that EPA will approve it.

Form Approved
OMB No. 2000-0228
Exp. 05/31/85

PETITION FOR MITIGATION

PLEASE PRINT CLEARLY OR TYPE

Name and Address of Importer	Make of Vehicle
	Model of Vehicle
Port of Entry	Model Year
Date of Entry	Vehicle Identification No.
Customs Entry Number	

TO: The U. S. Customs Service:

I have determined that I am unable to bring the vehicle described above, which I have imported under bond, into conformity with Federal emission requirements.   I hereby declare that this is the first nonconforming vehicle which I have imported into the United States and that it is being imported for my own personal use and not for commercial resale.   I request that at the end of the EPA compliance period I be assessed a penalty equal to one-quarter of the value of the bond posted at the time of importation and be permitted to retain possession of this vehicle in the United States.

I understand that this mitigated penalty applies only with respect to Federal emission requirements administered by the U. S. Environmental Protection Agency.   It does not relieve me of the obligation to comply with Federal safety requirements administered by the U. S. Department of Transportation or any applicable state or local emission-related requirements.   I further understand that I must pay any applicable import duty on this vehicle.

____
Signature of Importer

Subscribed and Sworn To Before Me

This______________Day of ________________________, 19______

Notary Public
My Commission Expires:______________________________

Mail this petition to:

Investigation/Imports Section
MOD (EN-340F)
U. S. Environmental Protection Agency
Washington, D C   20460

California Smog Check

Beginning April 20, 1984, California implemented auto inspections for smog in certain counties. The new testing is done by computer-controlled units. The regulations, procedures and laws essentially state that any direct import (not through a car dealer) two years old or less must be converted by a certified converter (smog and emissions). This is to ensure standards are being met.

Direct imports over two years old will still have to be converted, by any shop that can handle the work. They will still have to pass California smog and emissions tests in order to be registered.

Shops that are certified provide a form (new) guaranteeing that the car has been converted and has met California smog and emissions tests. This form is given instead of the smog certificate for first-time registration in the state.

These new provisions do not apply to "any motor vehicle having a certificate of conformity issued by the federal Environmental Protection Agency pursuant to the Federal Clean Air Act (42 U.S.C. Section 7401, et seq.) and originally registered in another state by a person who was a resident of that state for at least one year prior to the original registration, who subsequently establishes residence in this state, and who, upon registration of the vehicle in California, provides evidence satisfactory to the Department of Motor Vehicles of that previous residence and registration."

The two-year provision is a law, but will probably not be implemented until January 1987. In the meantime, check with the California DMV as to changes that may have occurred if you plan on taking a car into California.

The following information is to help you obtain your *SMOG CHECK CERTIFICATE* as easily as possible and to inform you about the many safeguards that have been built into this program.

If you live in California, the first thing to do is determine whether or not your car needs a *SMOG CHECK CERTIFICATE* before mailing your registration renewal forms and fees to the DMV.

If your car needs a *SMOG CHECK CERTIFICATE*, follow the directions outlined here, and when you have received your *CERTIFICATE*, mail it with your renewal forms and your check or money order to the DMV.

Your car's registration will expire approximately 45 days after you receive notice. The expiration date appears on your renewal notice. Make sure that you have your *SMOG CHECK CERTIFICATE* in time to return your registration renewal forms to the DMV before your car's registration expires.

If you have questions that are not answered here, you can call the State Bureau of Automotive Repair office nearest you.

Sacramento	(916) 366-5023
Pleasant Hill	(415) 798-3840
San Jose	(408) 277-1860
San Francisco	(415) 468-6700
Hayward	(415) 785-1961
Santa Rosa	(707) 576-2075
Fresno	(209) 445-5015
Ventura	(805) 654-4507
Santa Ana	(714) 558-4008
Fl Monte	(818) 575-7005
Upland	(714) 946-9641
Downey	(213) 861-0987
North Hollywood	(818) 982-2205
Riverside	(714) 781-4250
Inglewood	(213) 412-6111
Culver City	(213) 391-0355
San Diego	(619) 560-0114
Oceanside	(619) 439-0942

The "Important Notice" enclosed in the envelope with your registration renewal notice also lists the phone numbers of the eighteen offices. If there is no district office near you, phone toll-free 800-952-5210 for help.

Why does my car need a checkup?

Automobiles emit approximately half of the pollution that causes smog, and they emit nearly ninety-five percent of the invisible carbon monoxide that can cause serious health problems. Most of these dangerous automobile emissions are invisible, but it is true that even new cars can create serious pollution problems. Without smog inspections, people cannot tell if their cars are polluters. Minor repairs required in this inspection may cut pollutants by up to twenty-five percent.

Does my car require a smog check certificate?

In order for California to meet the requirements of the federal Clean Air Act, most Californians who live in areas where air pollution is a problem will need to obtain *SMOG CHECK CERTIFICATES* for their automobiles, light vans, and trucks every other year at the time when each vehicle's registration comes up for renewal.

If the registration renewal notice you received says *SMOG CERTIFICATE REQUIRED*, your vehicle is

IMPORTANT NOTICE

This is to alert you to the need for you to participate in *SMOG CHECK*, a new program designed to help California meet federal Clean Air Act requirements. *SMOG CHECK* inspections and repairs of emission control equipment on automobiles, light trucks and vans will improve air quality in areas of California where smog is a serious threat to health.

If the registration renewal notice you received in this envelope says *SMOG CERTIFICATE REQUIRED,* **the vehicle is due for inspection now,** and you must obtain a certificate before you can forward your renewal forms to the Department of Motor Vehicles. You have approximately 30 to 45 days to complete the process before your registration expires. The expiration date appears on your renewal notice.

The envelope in which this letter was mailed contains a brochure that explains *SMOG CHECK.* The brochure:

- Gives step-by-step instructions for those participating in the *SMOG CHECK* program.

- Explains how to determine if your vehicle is one of the few that is exempt from *SMOG CHECK.*

- Explains the program's costs and the consumer safeguards that are built into *SMOG CHECK.*

Local phone numbers you may call for further information about *SMOG CHECK* are listed on the back of this notice.

Scientists have determined that the *SMOG CHECK* program will enable us to achieve a significant decrease in automobile pollutants, which cause more than half of all our air pollution. Our health and the quality of life we enjoy depend upon our working together to make *SMOG CHECK* successful.

On behalf of the State of California, thank you for your participation in this important program.

due for inspection now unless it is exempt from the *SMOG CHECK* program.

If your car has been selected, please read on. Your registration expires in approximately thirty to forty-five days on the expiration date that appears on your renewal notice. You must obtain your *SMOG CHECK CERTIFICATE* before your registration expires. The penalties for driving an unregistered car can be severe and can amount to a twenty percent fee surcharge or a mandatory court appearance and even more costly fines.

If the renewal notice does not say *SMOG CERTIFICATE REQUIRED,* your inspection may be scheduled for registration renewal next year. You should register your car by sending in your renewal notice and fees, just as you have done in the past. However, I suggest you read on to see what you will be required to do when your turn comes.

Even if your registration renewal notice says *SMOG CERTIFICATE REQUIRED,* your vehicle is exempt from this program if any of the following is true.

A. The vehicle is more than twenty years old.
B. It is powered by anything other than gasoline. (This category includes all diesel powered vehicles, electric cars, cars run on pure methanol and ethyl alcohol.)
C. It is registered in one of the areas in California that does not meet designated federal Air Quality standards, but is garaged outside these areas. (If unsure, please check with your county Air Pollution Control District.)
D. Its gross vehicle weight rating is more than 8,500 pounds. Your vehicle's gross vehicle weight rating is recorded on the I.D. plate, usually attached to the front door frame on the driver's side.

If your vehicle is exempt, please note the reason on your registration renewal and return the notice to the DMV with your renewal fees. Please be sure you are giving correct information, as there are penalties for providing false information.

How does the program work?

If your car or truck needs a *SMOG CHECK CERTIFICATE,* here's what to do:

Drive your car or truck to any shop which shows the *SMOG CHECK* sign. Check the owner's manual for warranty instructions. If your car is under factory warranty, take the warranty information with you.

A trained mechanic will use specially designed computer-analyzers to measure your car's pollution. If your car is in good working order and its pollution (smog) control equipment works properly, you will be given a *SMOG CHECK CERTIFICATE* to mail to the DMV with your registration renewal form. It is primarily the computer-analyzer that determines if your car needs repair—not the mechanic. You will receive a report printed by the analyzer (see sample) that indicates why your car passed or why your car failed the *SMOG CHECK.*

If your car is not properly tuned, or if you have removed or tampered with the smog control equipment, the car must be repaired before you can receive your *SMOG CHECK CERTIFICATE.*

Remember, you have a choice. You may have your car repaired at the same shop where it was inspected (if that shop has a state license to do *SMOG CHECK* repairs), or you may take the computer printed report explaining why your car failed to any other repair shop that displays the *SMOG CHECK* sign.

How much does the program cost?

For the inspection, you will probably be charged by the smog check station for the inspection. If there is an inspection fee, it will be posted at the station. It is advisable to shop around, as the fee may vary from one station to another.

Some shops are licensed to do inspections only, and other shops are licensed to do both inspections and repairs. You may wish to ask about the shop's pricing policy, and find out whether or not you will have to pay for the reinspection if your car does not pass the first time and needs to be repaired.

For the repair (if needed), the mechanic is required to give you a written cost estimate. If the smog equipment on your car has not been removed, modified or tampered with, you will be required to spend no more than $50 to repair the car. (Adjustments and repairs often cost less.) If the smog equipment has been removed or tampered with, it must be restored before a smog certificate can be issued. The cost of this is not included in the $50 limit. There is a $6 processing fee for your car's *SMOG CHECK CERTIFICATE.* This is a charge by the State of California and is paid when your car passes the inspection to the mechanic or referee who inspects or repairs your car. The charge for the inspection is in addition to the $6 fee. Your registration will not be renewed without the *SMOG CHECK CERTIFICATE.*

What if my car doesn't pass inspection?

If your mechanic certifies that repairs costing more than $50 would be needed for your car to meet pollution standards, you can still get a *SMOG CHECK*

CERTIFICATE without spending more than $50 if: the smog equipment has not been removed or tampered with; state-required adjustments and minor repairs are made to lower pollution levels; all other repairs possible within the $50 cost limit have been made; and the repairs that are made positively lower emission levels. The computer-analyzer will make this determination.

If the mechanic cannot reduce your car's pollution levels, you will be referred to a state-qualified referee station before the *SMOG CHECK CERTIFICATE* is issued. There is no additional charge for the referee's services.

If you repair the car yourself, or have it repaired by a mechanic not qualified by the state, the $50 limit does not apply. You may receive a *SMOG CHECK CERTIFICATE* only if your car meets the appropriate pollution standards, or a state referee confirms further improvement is impossible.

What kinds of repairs might my car need?

Bureau of Automotive Repair engineers estimate that most vehicles that fail *SMOG CHECK* inspections will need minor, inexpensive repairs or adjustments. A clogged air filter, a vacuum leak, spark plugs or wires that need cleaning or replacing, or a carburetor mixture that is too rich are likely to cause your car to fail inspection. Repairing these faults will probably make your car run more efficiently on less gasoline, and that will save you money in the long run.

What is this computer-analyzer that will be used to test my car?

The analyzer is a new instrument, designed to meet strict State of California requirements. It is tamper resistant and designed for accuracy. Remember, it is the analyzer, not the mechanic, that determines whether or not your car can pass inspection and whether or not repair work is necessary. The analyzer has a built-in computer that continually monitors the machine's accuracy. If the analyzer becomes inaccurate, or if it is tampered with, the computer will automatically turn the machine off so that it cannot produce a false test of your car's condition. In addition, the analyzer and the inspection stations are monitored regularly by state authorized inspectors.

How do I know that the mechanic who inspects and repairs my car is competent and honest?

All mechanics authorized to inspect and repair cars for this program must pass a strict training pro-

IMPORTANT! RETURN THIS DOCUMENT WITH YOUR VEHICLE REGISTRATION

CERTIFICATE OF COMPLIANCE · MOTOR VEHICLE POLLUTION CONTROL

DEPARTMENT OF Consumer Affairs — BUREAU OF AUTOMOTIVE REPAIR

VEHICLE LICENSE NUMBER

A 1866595

LAST THREE DIGITS OF VEHICLE ID NUMBER: 2 0 2

IF METHANOL POWERED, CHECK BOX ☐

I certify, under penalty of perjury under the laws of the State of California, that the above described vehicle has been inspected in compliance with the requirements of Chapter 5, part 5, Division 26, of the California Health and Safety Code and that the above vehicle is in compliance with applicable laws and regulations. This certificate is valid for ninety days from the date of issuance.

LICENSED INSPECTOR'S SIGNATURE

INSPECTOR'S LICENSE NUMBER
79-1 / N O 94417

STATION LICENSE NUMBER
RD 094417

DATE OF ISSUANCE
5/12/84

```
**********************************

CALIFORNIA VEHICLE INSPECTION REPORT

**********************************

YOUR VEHICLE'S SMOG TEST MEANS CLEANER
AIR FOR US ALL.  THANK YOU FOR HELPING.

RESULTS OF YOUR INSPECTION
**************************


PASSED
------


CONGRATULATIONS
YOUR VEHICLE PASSED
THE CALIFORNIA EMISSION INSPECTION

********************************************

CERTIFICATE OF COMPLIANCE NUMBER
A1866595C

********************************************


INITIAL INSPECTION

********************************************

ANTI-SMOG EQUIPMENT INSPECTION
------------------------------

POSITIVE CRANKCASE VENTILATION       PASS
AIR INJECTION SYSTEM                  PASS
FUEL EVAPORATION SYSTEM               PASS
CARBURETOR/FUEL INJECTION             PASS


ENGINE SYSTEM CHECK
-------------------

ENGINE WARNING LIGHTS                 PASS
IGNITION TIMING                       N/A
EGR TEST                              N/A


IDLE EMISSION RESULTS
---------------------
         STANDARDS              MEASURED
HC       200 PPM      PASS      73 PPM
CO       3.50 %       PASS      1.61 %
CO2                              14.00 %
RPM                              1008 RPM


HIGH RPM EMISSION RESULTS
-------------------------
         STANDARDS              MEASURED
HC       NONE                   57 PPM
CO       NONE                   3.08 %
CO2                             13.15 %
RPM                             2546 RPM

********************************************


VEHICLE INFORMATION
-------------------

LICENSE NUMBER              F STRNYU
MAKE                        PORS
YEAR                        76
NUMBER OF CYLINDERS         6
ENGINE SIZE                 3.0 LI
ODOMETER                    139719
VEHICLE TYPE                PASSENGER CAR
```

gram administered by the State of California. In addition, their repair work is monitored by state inspectors and quality assurance experts. The State Referee program is another safeguard, and the mechanics know that if they act improperly, the State of California will impose fines of up to $500 per day, and may also suspend them from the program.

How do I know my car really needs the repairs the inspector tells me it must have?

If your car fails the inspection, the computer-analyzer will produce a printed report that indicates the reasons for the failure. You should discuss this report with your mechanic before you authorize repairs. The mechanic must give you a written estimate of repairs before doing any work. You must be given a detailed copy of the repair bill when the work is finished.

What can I do if I think my car has not been repaired properly?

If you have a problem you cannot resolve with the shop manager, you may call for a State of California Bureau of Automotive Repair inspector to investigate your complaint. To do so, please see your local phone directory for the number of the Bureau's nearest office. The inspector may ask you to take your car to a State Referee to have the work checked.

What if my car is new and still under warranty, and it doesn't pass inspection?

Your car's manufacturer may have to pay for some or all of the repair work if your car is less than five years old and has been driven fewer than 50,000 miles. If your car fails inspection, check your owners manual before you have any repair work done. Please remember, however, that you, and not the manufacturer, are responsible for the routine, required maintenance outlined in your manual.

How can I be sure I spend as little money as possible to obtain my *SMOG CHECK CERTIFICATE*?

Everyone is required to pay the $6 *SMOG CHECK CERTIFICATE* fee, but each inspection and repair shop may set its own fees as long as the charge for repairs is not more than $50. Shop around before you decide where to take your car for inspection and repairs.

What benefits will the inspection program provide for California?

By reducing smog, this program will provide a healthier place to live. Children and senior citizens, in particular, suffer from smog-related illnesses, but everyone will be healthier when our air is cleaner. It will also save us money. Air pollution costs millions of dollars for health care, lost time on the job and damaged crops for which we all pay.

California (DMV) policies

The following DMV policies are in effect for those cars being brought into California.

STATE OF CALIFORNIA
DEPARTMENT OF MOTOR VEHICLES
DIVISION OF REGISTRATION AND INVESTIGATIVE SERVICES

PROCEDURAL MEMO   P-85-13   April 8, 1985

TO   : DEALERS, INVESTIGATIVE SERVICES PERSONNEL, BANKS, FINANCE
          COMPANIES AND ALL HOLDERS OF THE MANUAL OF REGISTRATION
          PROCEDURES

FROM   : ROGER E. HAGEN, CHIEF, REGISTRATION AND INVESTIGATIVE SERVICES

SUBJECT: NON-U.S. MODEL VEHICLES

A large number of applications for registration of vehicles that were not
manufactured for use in the United States or California are currently
being reviewed in Headquarters. As part of the review process, it was
discovered that certain items were often omitted. This memo serves as a
reminder and an update regarding imported vehicles.

    I. <u>Ownership Documents</u>

Every vehicle manufactured for sale in Germany (i.e., Non-U.S.
model) has a Fahrzeugbrief. German vehicles manufactured for
sale in the United States or those United States version
vehicles ordered by American tourists for delivery in Germany
will have a Manufacturer's Statement of Origin (MSO) issued by
the factory. The tourist who uses the vehicle in Europe
surrenders the MSO to receive an international registration
called an <u>Internationaler Zulassungsschien</u>. Therefore, those
applications containing the Fahrzeugbrief instead of the MSO
or International Registration are for <u>non-U.S.</u> model
vehicles. <u>Registration is prohibited if the mileage is less
than 7500 miles, unless the owner qualifies for one of the
exemptions listed in Section 43151 of the Health and Safety
Code.</u> (See Reg. 256F - Attachment 2).

    II. <u>Fahrzeugbrief</u>

The Fahrzeugbrief is a manufacturer-issued certificate of
title which in Germany performs the function of both the MSO
and the certificate of title. A vehicle manufactured in
Germany, but intended for sale in another European country
will not have a Fahrzeugbrief, but will have titling documents
from the country of sale.

On the face of the Fahrzeugbrief are spaces for four entries
of the owners' names. These entries are made by the German
authorities when the owner's name is officially recorded. The
German authorities sign and date the entry and stamp the
document with their official seal. The presence of the seal

authenticates the entry. **These represent a recording of
ownership with the German "DMV"; they are not bills of sale.**

In many instances, the new owner's name is being typed in this
space on the Fahrzeugbrief in an attempt to transfer
ownership. In the example shown in Attachment 1, the first
entry is valid but a bill of sale from Irrschick Schneeberger
to Best Buy would be required to complete the chain of
ownership.

III. <u>Value of Conversion</u>

A Certificate of Cost or Value (reverse of Reg. 343
Application for Registration) is completed by an individual
who purchases a nonresident or imported vehicle. When an
imported vehicle has been modified after arrival in this
country to meet federal emissions and safety regulations, the
cost of the modification is to be shown on the reverse of the
343 as a cost of alteration. This amount will be added to the
purchase amount to determine the vehicle license fee class.

IV. <u>Reg. 346 - Use Tax Statement for a Vehicle Imported From a
Foreign Country</u>

This form is to be completed when foreign documents are
submitted and the use tax is waived because the vehicle was
<u>operated</u> for 91 or more days in a foreign country. Tax paid
to a foreign country may not be applied to use tax owed to
California.

V. <u>Compliance With California and Federal Emissions and Safety
Requirements</u>

A. Statement of Facts (Reg. 256F)

The Statement of Facts (Reg. 256F, Attachment 2) has been
modified in an effort to clarify the requirements of the
program. It is now entitled, **"Statement of Facts, New,
Nonresident or Imported Vehicle."** **It must be completed on
<u>all</u> applications for original registration of (1) vehicles
with less than 7500 odometer miles, and (2) vehicles with
7500 odometer miles or more that are accompanied by
registration or ownership documents from a foreign country.**

<u>NOTE</u>: It will be a rare situation when an applicant can
justify registering a non-U.S. model vehicle in California
with less than 7500 miles.

Sections 1 and 2 of the Reg. 256F have been keyed to the odometer reading of the vehicle, as follows:

1.   Odometer reading of less than 7500 miles.

This part of the form must be completed for the original registration of any vehicle with less than 7500 miles (12,070 kilometers). If box 1(a) is marked, no other declarations must be made except to date and sign the form at the bottom. A Certificate of Compliance must be submitted with the application, unless the vehicle is diesel or electric-powered, or a motorcycle.

If boxes 1(b) or 1(c) are marked, the sections under box 1(d) must also be completed. A Certificate of Compliance or Noncompliance must be submitted. If box 1(c) is marked, clearance letters from EPA and DOT must be submitted for 1968 and later year models before the application can be cleared for issuance of documents and plates.

2.   Odometer reading of 7500 miles or more

This part of the form must be completed for the original registration of any vehicle with 7500 miles or more that is accompanied by foreign ownership or registration documents. If box 2(a) is marked, no other declarations must be made except to date and sign the form at the bottom. A Certificate of Compliance must be submitted with the application, unless the vehicle is diesel or electric-powered, a motorcycle, or a year model 1964 or prior.

If box 2(b) is marked, a Certificate of Compliance must be submitted with the application, unless the vehicle is diesel or electric-powered, a motorcycle, or a year model 1964 or prior. EPA and DOT clearance letters must be submitted for 1968 and later year models.

B.   Issuance of Permits

A Temporary Operating Permit (Reg. 19) can be issued for 120 days, if the applicant deposits the fees due, submits a copy of the Motor Vehicle Emission Report Form, the Statement of Compliance form, and a vehicle verification which indicates odometer mileage. (ALL THREE ITEMS MUST BE SUBMITTED BEFORE THE 120-DAY TEMPORARY OPERATING PERMIT CAN BE ISSUED).

If the applicant is not going to be able to bring the
vehicle into compliance, a Temporary Operating Permit
valid for ten days may be issued (without the Motor
Vehicle Emission Report Form or the Statement of
Compliance form) for the purpose of removing the vehicle
from California, if the applicant deposits the fees due.
If fees have not become due, a One Trip Permit may be
issued for the purpose of removing the vehicle from
California.

A Special No Fee Moving Permit (Reg. 172) may be issued
under the conditions specified in Chapter 9 of the
Registration Manual if fees have not become due, and the
applicant needs to move the vehicle for the purpose of
completing alterations that will bring the vehicle into
compliance. This permit also may be issued in lieu of a
One-Trip Permit for removing the vehicle from California,
if the conditions specified in Chapter 9 are met.

VI.   Telephone Numbers

Please use the following telephone numbers instead of those
listed in Procedural Memo P-84-17:

Environmental Protection Agency (EPA)

San Francisco   (415) 974-8067
Washington, D. C.   (202) 382-2505

National Highway Traffic Safety Administration (NHTSA)

San Francisco   (415) 974-9840
Washington, D. C.   (202) 426-1693

VII.   Import Vehicle Check Sheet

An Imported Vehicle List (Attachment 3) has been prepared to
assist you when foreign documents are submitted with an
application.

If you have any questions, please contact Jeanine Counselman at
(916) 323-0247.

ROGER E. HAGEN
Chief

IMPORT VEHICLES WITH UNDER 7500 MILES

Documents Needed:

1. Valid titling document or a bond (see Chapter 16 of the Registration
    Manual). A European community statement of origin is not a titling
    document.

2. Bills of sale showing the chain of ownership (e.g., back to owner
    recorded by German authorities).

3. Verification that includes an odometer reading. (Required before a
    permit can be issued).

4. Reg. 256F with one of the boxes under #1 checked. May not check the
    box that says it is factory equipped if a Fahrzeugbrief is attached.
    The Fahrzeugbrief accompanies vehicles made for use in Germany. If
    one of the other exemptions is checked, then EPA and DOT clearance
    letters must be submitted for 1968 and later year models..

    If "none of the above" is marked under question #1 of the Reg. 256F
    or if the applicant refuses to complete the form, then registration
    is to be refused. See Registration Manual 10.100b for additional
    instructions.

5. Smog certificate of Compliance or Non-Compliance, as appropriate
    (unless diesel, electric powered or a motorcycle).

6. Reg. 346, Use Tax Statement for a Vehicle Imported From a Foreign
    Country is needed if tax is not collected because the vehicle was
    operated in Europe for 91 or more days.

7. EPA and DOT Clearance letters if the vehicle was not factory equipped
    to meet California emission standards and U.S. Safety regulations.
    (Required before plates can be issued).

8. EPA form OMB 2000-0228 and DOT form OMB 2127-0012 must be submitted
    before a 120-day permit can be issued if vehicle was not factory
    equipped but does qualify under exemptions for form 256F.

Documents needed:

1. Valid titling document or a bond (see Chapter 16 of the Registration Manual).

2. Bills of sale showing the chain of ownership (e.g., back to owner recorded by German authorities).

3. Verification that includes an odometer reading. (Required before a permit can be issued).

4. Reg. 256F with one of the boxes under #2 checked. Only owners of vehicles bought in Europe, but made for the U. S. market, may mark the first box. A Fahrzeugbrief indicates the vehicle was not made for the U. S. market. If the second box is marked, then clearance letters from EPA and DOT are needed for 1968 and later year models.

   If the applicant refuses to complete the Reg. 256F or refuses to submit EPA and DOT clearance letters are required, then registration is to be refused. See Registration Manual 10.100b for additional instructions.

5 Smog certificate showing compliance (unless diesel, electric powered or a motorcycle).

   Reg. 346, Use Tax Statement for a Vehicle Imported from a Foreign Country is needed if tax is not collected because the vehicle was operated for 91 or more days in Europe.

7. EPA and DOT Clearance letters if the vehicle was modified after importation. (Required before plates can be issued)

8. EPA form OMB 2000-0228 and DOT form OMB 2127-0012 must be submitted before a 120-day permit can be issued if vehicle was modified after importation.

<table>
<tr><td colspan="2">STATE OF CALIFORNIA
DEPARTMENT OF MOTOR VEHICLES

CERTIFICATION OF PURCHASE PRICE

A   All Vehicles and Vessels (Except Trailer Coaches)</td><td>MAKE OF VEHICLE OR VESSEL BUILDER

YEAR MODEL</td></tr>
</table>

VEHICLE OR HULL IDENTIFICATION NUMBER | VEHICLE LIC NO OR VESSEL CF NO

FOR VESSELS ONLY: LENGTH   FT   IN | PROPULSION | HULL MATERIAL | HULL TYPE

NAME OF PURCHASER (PLEASE PRINT—LAST, FIRST, MIDDLE)

ADDRESS

CITY   STATE   ZIP

LOCATION WHERE VESSEL IS KEPT (ADDRESS OR MARINA) OR WHERE VEHICLE IS PRINCIPALLY USED IF OTHER THAN RESIDENCE ADDRESS

CITY   COUNTY

The above described vehicle was purchased on ________________ from
DATE

NAME OF SELLER (PLEASE PRINT—LAST, FIRST, MIDDLE)

ADDRESS

CITY   STATE   ZIP

TOTAL PURCHASE PRICE (Price includes cash, the amount of any loan and/or the value of any property, vehicle or vessel given in trade.) $

☐ **Check this box if the total price shown is the price of the vessel/trailer combination.**

NOTE: THIS CERTIFICATE WILL BE REVIEWED BY THE STATE BOARD OF EQUALIZATION, AND THE FACTS SUBMITTED HEREON MAY BE SUBJECT TO VERIFICATION.

Executed on ____________ at ________________ , __________
DATE   CITY   STATE

I certify under penalty of perjury that the foregoing is true and correct.

Signature   **X** __________________________

TAX BASIS
    Vehicles - Residence or allocation county
    Vessels   - Situs county or residence county, if no situs

RATE OF TAX
    6½% Counties of Alameda, Contra Costa, Los Angeles, San Francisco, San Mateo, Santa Cruz, and Santa Clara
    6%   All other counties

HOW TO COMPUTE THE TAX DUE. Multiply the purchase price by .06 or .065 whichever applies. Round out to the nearest dollar.

STATE, LOCAL AND TRANSIT DISTRICT USE TAX DUE $

REG. 347 (REV. 10/82)

STATEMENT OF FACTS
NEW, NONRESIDENT OR IMPORTED VEHICLE

VEHICLE I.D. NUMBER	LICENSE NUMBER
ENGINE NUMBER (MOTORCYCLES)	VEHICLE NAME

Regarding the above: *(Check (   ) the following statements which apply.)*

1. ☐ ODOMETER **LESS THAN** 7500 MILES (12,070 kilometers): This application contains registration or ownership documents from **another state** or a **foreign country** *and:*
   (If this box is checked, one or more of the following must also be checked.)

   a. ☐ This vehicle is factory-equipped to meet California emission standards and U.S. safety regulations.
   (Certificate of Compliance required, unless diesel or electric powered, or a motorcycle.)

   b. ☐ At the time of entry into California, this vehicle was equipped to meet federal emission and safety regulations only.
   (Certificate of Compliance of Noncompliance acceptable, only if "Exemption" section (d) below is also completed.)

   c. ☐ As modified after entry into California, this vehicle meets federal emission and safety regulations only. COST OF MODIFICATION $ ___________________ .
   (Certificate of Compliance or Noncompliance acceptable, ONLY if "Exemption" section (d) below is also completed.)
   (EPA and DOT clearance letters required for 1968 and later year model vehicles.)

   d. ☐ EXEMPTION
   - ☐ When I acquired this vehicle, I was a resident of a country or state **other** than California.
   - ☐ This vehicle was acquired:
     - ☐ as a result of an inheritance.
     - ☐ as a result of a divorce, dissolution, or legal separation entered by a court of competent jurisdiction.
     - ☐ to replace a vehicle that was damaged or became inoperative beyond reasonable repair or was stolen while out of state.

   e. ☐ None of the above (See "Note" below.)

2. ☐ ODOMETER 7500 MILES **OR MORE** (12,070 kilometers): This application contains registration or ownership documents from a **foreign country**, *and:*
   (If this box is checked, one of the following must also be checked.)

   a. ☐ As imported, this vehicle conforms to all applicable federal emission and safety regulations in effect on the date of its importation.
   (Certificate of Compliance required for 1965 and later models, unless diesel or electric powered, or a motorcycle.)

   b. ☐ As modified after importation, this vehicle conforms to all applicable federal motor vehicle emissions and safety regulations in effect on the date of its importation. COST OF MODIFICATION $ _______________________
   (Certificate of Compliance required for 1965 and later models, unless diesel or electric powered, or a motorcycle.)
   (EPA and DOT Clearance letters required for 1968 and later year model vehicles.)

VEHICLE CUSTOMS ENTRY NO. *(If avail.)*	DATE OF ENTRY *(If avail.)*	PORT OF ENTRY *(If avail.)*

I certify under penalty of perjury that the foregoing is true and correct.

EXECUTED ON *(DATE)*	AT *(CITY AND STATE)*

SIGNATURE **X**	DAYTIME TELEPHONE NUMBER ( )

> **NOTE:** California law prohibits the registration by California residents of vehicles which have less than 7500 odometer miles and which have not been certified by the Air Resources Board, unless exempted by one of the conditions above (VC 4000b, H & S 43151). A Certificate of Compliance (**not** a Certificate of Noncompliance) from a licensed inspection station is the only acceptable evidence of certification by the Air Resources Board.
>
> If a Certificate of Compliance cannot be obtained for your vehicle and you do not qualify for one of the exemptions above, you cannot register the vehicle. If it has not been operated in a manner to cause fees to become due, you may purchase a One Trip Permit to remove the vehicle from California.

REG. 256F (REV 2 /85)

CALIFORNIA LICENSE NO

APPLICATION FOR REGISTRATION

☐ Reflectorized
Plates

☐ N — New
☐ O — Old (Used)
☐ R — Non-resident

TYPE PLATE

DATE FEES DUE	MONTH / DAY / YEAR	REG. EXP.	MONTH / DAY / YEAR	NRM

VEHICLE I D NO — WF

M/C ENGINE NO OR ADD'L I D NO | EQUIPMENT NO | TYPE LICENSE — RF / LF

MAKE | BODY TYPE | COMPRESSION RATIO TO 1 | BODY TYPE ABBR. — PEN

IF KNOWN, DATE FIRST SOLD AS A NEW VEHICLE | MONTH / DAY / YEAR | COST VALUE | VLF CLASS | YR. — 01

FOR TRAILER COACHES ONLY | LENGTH IN INCHES ( ) | WIDTH IN INCHES ( ) | TYPE VEH. | TYPE BODY — 02 / 03

YR MODEL | MOTIVE POWER | NO OF AXLES | UNLADEN WEIGHT | WT CODE | SMOG CODE — 04

I AM NOW RESIDING IN THE COUNTY OF | P H CODE | REG. CO | ALLOC CO — 05 / UT

RECEIPT NO. | DATE FEE REC | RATE CLK. — TOT

Registered Owner(s) *(Print True Name(s))*
(1) LAST — FIRST — MIDDLE
(2) AND ☐ OR ☐ LAST — FIRST — MIDDLE

BUSINESS OR RESIDENCE ADDRESS — APT NO.

CITY — ZIP CODE

LIENHOLDER (NAME OF THE COMPANY OR INDIVIDUAL WHO NOW HAS A LIEN ON THIS VEHICLE. IF NONE, SO STATE.) *(PRINT TRUE NAME)*

INITIALS

BUSINESS OR RESIDENCE ADDRESS

CITY — STATE — ZIP CODE

CERTIFICATE OF COST OR VALUE

Date Purchased or Acquired — Cost

A. Cost of vehicle purchased or acquired as a complete vehicle _________ $ _______
Cost of additions and/or alterations (Include cost of installation) .... _________ $ _______

Total cost of vehicle .... $ _______
B. Total present value of complete vehicle (assembled, special constructed or reconstructed vehicle) include labor repair and modification cost .... $ _______

NOTE: The total cost or value of the vehicle must include the cost of the basic vehicle, value of any trade-in, and all accessories and leased equipment permanently attached. Cost does not include sales tax, insurance or finance charges.

PLEASE COMPLETE REVERSE SIDE.

FOR DEPARTMENT USE ONLY

NAME OF STATE NOTIFIED BY MAIL	PLATE NO.	TAKEN UP
		NONE 1 2

REG 343 (REV 8/84) — 84 33738

REGISTRATION QUESTIONNAIRE

ALL APPLICANTS, PLEASE ANSWER THE FOLLOWING QUESTIONS:

A vehicle dealer need answer only questions 1, 2 and 3 and the information on the front.

1. Will this vehicle be used for hire to transport persons? .... ☐ Yes ☐ No

2. Do you want reflectorized license plates? (Addl. $5) .... ☐ Yes ☐ No

3. I certify that the odometer reading of this vehicle upon sale is _______________
   ☐ miles ☐ kilometers (If less than 7,500 miles or 12,070 kilometers, Reg. 256F must be completed and attached.)

4. Date vehicle first operated in California .... Month _____ Day _____ Year _____

5. Date vehicle first entered California .... Month _____ Day _____ Year _____

6. If this vehicle was previously registered:

   a. It was last registered in ____ for 19 _____
      State or Country

   b. You were a resident of ____
      State or Country

7. Except for any accompanying titles, are there any outstanding titles for this vehicle issued by any state or country? .... ☐ Yes ☐ No

8. Is this vehicle now being used as security for any lien other than the lien shown (if any) on the reverse side of this application? .... ☐ Yes ☐ No

IF THIS IS AN OUT-OF-STATE VEHICLE, PLEASE ANSWER:

9. Are you a resident of California? .... ☐ Yes ☐ No

   If "Yes" when did you become a resident? .... Month _____ Day _____ Year _____

10. Are you gainfully employed or in business in California? .... ☐ Yes ☐ No
    If "Yes" when did you become gainfully employed or enter into business

    in California? .... Month _____ Day _____ Year _____

IF THIS IS A FOREIGN COUNTRY REGISTERED VEHICLE, PLEASE COMPLETE:

11. ☐ I request retention of my surrendered foreign license plate(s) issued to the above

    described vehicle by the country of _______________________________________

    The plate(s) will be retained as a souvenir and will not be affixed to any vehicle at any time.

NOTE: IF THE APPLICATION CONTAINS FOREIGN OWNERSHIP OR REGISTRATION DOCUMENTS, REG. 256G MUST BE COMPLETED.

MILITARY SERVICE INFORMATION

12. Are you on active duty as a member of the U.S Armed Forces? ...... ☐ Yes ☐ No
    If "Yes" and you are not a resident of California, ask for and complete Department form Reg. 344.

13 When this vehicle was last licensed, were you on active duty as a member of the U.S. Armed Forces? .... ☐ Yes ☐ No

    If "Yes", in what state or country were you stationed? _______________________

IMPORTANT NOTICE

Your present registration is valid until ______________ . Renew on or before ______________ to avoid penalties. If the vehicle is sold or transferred, registration fees will be due immediately.

Office _________________________________ Rate Clerk _________________________________

Executed on ______________ at _________________________ , _________________________
          DATE   CITY   STATE

I/We certify under penalty of perjury that the statements made in this application are true and correct.

Signature(s)
of above
Registered
Owner(s)

(1) **X** ____

(2) **X** ____

DAYTIME TELEPHONE NO

( ) ____

EPA-certified test centers in California

Automotive Environmental Systems Inc.
7300 Bolsa Avenue
Westminster, CA 92683
(714) 897-0333

Custom Engineering
Performance and Emission Lab.
7091-A Belgrave Avenue
Garden Grove, CA 92641
(714) 891-5704

Fairway Environmental Eng.
3032 Kashiwa Street
Torrance, CA 90505
(213) 775-7618

Olson Engineering Inc.
15442 Chemical Lane
Huntington Beach, CA 93649
(714) 891-4821

Chapter 6

DOT requirements

Any auto imported into the United States must meet and conform to specifications according to US laws, as administered by the Department of Transportation (DOT). All autos imported by foreign manufacturers meet US specifications or they cannot be imported (since they are sold in the United States, these autos are manufactured to meet US specifications). Whereas, in most cases, autos purchased as used from the country of origin usually have not been manufactured to meet DOT requirements. These specifications, for the most part, are related to safety items such as side lights, headlights, seat belts, tires and protective devices. The foreign auto you purchase may not have any of those items or have only a few that meet DOT specifications. Information concerning changes in specifications can be obtained by writing to the Department of Transportation, National Highway Traffic Safety Administration, Office of Vehicle Safety Compliance (NEF-32CUS), 400 7th Street, SW, Room 6100, Washington, D.C. 20590.

The DOT gives the owner of the auto 120 days after importation to conform to its specifications. An extension of sixty days is provided if the conformation cannot be accomplished within that time period and there is a valid reason for not meeting the originally imposed time limit. The auto must be conformed or US customs will demand the bond or the auto or both. If it is not conformed, the auto is then subject to exportation back to the country of its origin or will be destroyed by US customs.

The following form is completed at the time of submission of import to US customs. It (O.M.B. No. 04-R2403) is sent by US customs to the DOT informing the agency of your importation of an auto.

Among the following is a sample DOT package (except O.M.B. Form 2127-0012 which cannot be reproduced). Completion of entry forms through the US customs automatically triggers DOT to send the package. In this package are the following: cover letter from DOT director, specific items to be conformed, general guide and summary description of standards.

If your auto has already conformed to meet US DOT requirements, it will have proper labels attached both for emissions (EPA) and for DOT, and conformation will not be required. However, you should be aware that it is unlikely that if the car was conformed in the country of origin that it was done correctly. Experience has proven that the shops in the country of origin may not know what the specifications or requirements are, as to EPA and DOT. Be prepared to have work done over when the car arrives in the United States.

DEPARTMENT OF TRANSPORTATION
NATIONAL HIGHWAY TRAFFIC SAFETY ADMINISTRATION

**IMPORTATION OF MOTOR VEHICLES AND MOTOR VEHICLE EQUIPMENT
SUBJECT TO FEDERAL MOTOR VEHICLE SAFETY STANDARDS**
(P.L. 89-563 SECTS. 108 AND 114, 19 C.F.R. 12.80)

FORM APPROVED
O.M.B. No. 04-R2403

This report is required by law and regulation (P.L. 89-563 and 19 C.F.R. 12.80). Failure to report will result in the refusal of entry of the vehicle(s) or equipment into the U.S.

PORT OF ENTRY	PORT CODE NUMBER	CUSTOMS ENTRY NUMBER AND DATE

IMPORT VESSEL OR CARRIER	MAKE OF MOTOR VEHICLE

MODEL	MODEL YEAR	BODY STYLE

CHASSIS SERIAL NUMBER	ENGINE NUMBER

DESCRIPTION OF MERCHANDISE IF MOTOR VEHICLE EQUIPMENT RATHER THAN A MOTOR VEHICLE IS BEING ENTERED ON THIS ENTRY

I DECLARE that the motor vehicle or equipment item (merchandise hereafter) described above is being offered for importation under the provisions of Title 19, Code of Federal Regulations, Part 12.80 as indicated by the section checked below:

☐ 1. Such merchandise was manufactured on a date when there were no applicable standards in effect. (i.e., motorcycles before 1/1/69; all others before 1/1/68). (12.80(b)(1)(i))

☐ 2. Such merchandise conforms to all applicable safety standards and bears a certification label affixed by its original manufacturer in accordance with P.L. 89-563, Section 114 (15 U.S.C. 1403) and regulations issued thereunder (41 CFR Parts 555, 567 or 568). (12.80(b)(1)(ii))

☒ 3. Such merchandise was not manufactured in conformity with all applicable safety standards, but has been or will be brought into conformity with such standards as evidenced by a true and complete statement to be submitted by the importer or consignee to the Administrator, National Highway Traffic Safety Administration (NHTSA) NEF-32, within 120 days or such additional time as may be agreed to by the Administrator, NHTSA, for good cause shown, but within the time frame set forth in 19 CFR 12.80(e)(2) (copy on reverse side of this form). Such statement shall identify the manufacturer, contractor, or other person who has brought the merchandise into conformity with such standards and shall describe the exact nature and extent of the work performed. It is further declared that the merchandise will not be sold or offered for sale until the bond required for 12.80(e)(1) shall have been released. (12.80(b)(1)(iii))

☐ 4. It is intended solely for export and such merchandise and the outside of its container, if any, are so labeled. (12.80(b)(1)(iv))

☐ 5. I am a nonresident of the United States and am importing the merchandise for personal use for a period not to exceed one year from the date of entry and I will not sell it within the United States. My Passport Number is: _______________ and was issued by (Country) _______________ (12.80(b)(1)(v))

☐ 6. I am a member of the armed forces of a *foreign* country, or a member of the Secretariat of a public international organization and so designated under the International Organization Immunities Act (22 U.S.C. 288), as listed in 19 CFR 148.87, on assignment in the United States, or a member of the personnel of a foreign government on assignment in the United States who comes within the class of persons for whom free entry of vehicles has been authorized by the Department of State and I am importing the merchandise for purposes other than resale. A copy of my official orders to assignment within the United States is attached. (12.80(b)(1)(vi))

☐ 7. I am importing the merchandise solely for purposes of ☐ show, ☐ test, ☐ experiment, ☐ competition (for purposes of this declaration, competition vehicles are those originally manufactured or modified prior to entry for competition use only), ☐ repairs or alterations, in accordance with the attached statement which describes fully the use and final disposition to be made of the merchandise. I understand that of the above, only vehicles entered for test or experiment may be licensed or used on the public roads and then only where such use is an integral part of the test or experiment described in the attached statement in which case the vehicle may be licensed or used on the public roads for a period not to exceed one year. Such use may be made for two additional years upon application to and approval by the Administrator, NHTSA. (12.80(b)(1)(vii)) (12.80(b)(2))

☐ 8. Such vehicle was not manufactured primarily for use on the public roads and is not a "motor vehicle" as defined in Section 102 of the Act (15 U.S.C. 1391). (12.80(b)(1)(viii))

☐ 9. Such vehicle is an incomplete vehicle as defined in 49 CFR Part 568. (12.80(b)(1)(ix))

PRINTED OR TYPED NAME OF IMPORTER	IMPORTER'S ADDRESS (Street, City, State, Zip Code)

PRINTED OR TYPED NAME OF DECLARANT (Legal Agent, including Customhouse Brokers)	DECLARANT'S ADDRESS (Street, City, State, Zip Code)

DECLARANT'S CAPACITY	DECLARANT'S SIGNATURE	DATE

HS Form 7 (Rev. 11/78)   Previou   obsolete.

82

PCI 8306-348-1

1

L.

IN REPLY REFER TO:

NEF-32CUS

Dear Importer:

You have imported the vehicle shown on the computerized sheet, Enclosure 1.

Sections 12.80(b)(1)(iii) and 12.80(e) of Title 19, Code of Federal Regulations, require that within 120 days of the date of entry you submit to this office a statement substantiating that the vehicle has been brought into conformity with all applicable Federal Motor Vehicle Safety Standards (FMVSS); if additional time is granted, the statement must reach this office in sufficient time to allow presentation to the District Director of Customs of a bond release letter within 180 days from the date of entry. For proper identification, your statement and every enclosure must include the chassis serial number and the PCI number shown above. Your statement must also identify the manufacturer, contractor, or other person who has brought the vehicle into conformity and must describe the exact nature and extent of the work performed with respect to the FMVSS which are listed on Enclosure 1. If this statement is not submitted within the time specified above, section 12.80(e)(2) requires that the vehicle be redelivered to the District Director of Customs at the port of entry.

Specific guidance on the requirements of the FMVSS is given on Enclosure 2 (Form HS-189). This form does not specify the complete or detailed requirements of the FMVSS, but only indicates the areas of apparent noncompliance which normally exist on motor vehicles not manufactured for the U.S. market. We advise that you consult the manufacturer's representative in the United States before attempting to bring your vehicle into conformity, particularly if you have imported a model or type which the manufacturer does not sell in the United States. You should note that for some requirements dealing with crash survivability, specifically FMVSS Nos. 203, 204, 207, 208, 210, 214, 216, 219, and 301, where applicable, (see Enclosure 1), proof of conformance is difficult to achieve without the manufacturer's compliance statement and in the event that you are unable to substantiate conformance, this agency will press for redelivery and export of the vehicle.

Upon review of your statement, the National Highway Traffic Safety
Administration may wish to verify its accuracy by requiring you to make
your vehicle available for an inspection to insure that it has, in fact,
been brought into conformity with all applicable FMVSS and that you have
not violated the National Traffic and Motor Vehicle Safety Act of 1966
(15 U.S.C. 1381 et seq.).

Failure to substantiate that the vehicle has been brought into conformity
within the allowed time renders you liable for imposition of a civil
penalty of up to $1,000 and/or assessment of liquidated damages in the
amount of the value of the vehicle, pursuant to the entry bond required by
section 12.80(e). You are also reminded that under section
12.80(b)(1)(iii) you may not sell the vehicle or offer it for sale prior to
release of the bond. A copy of Title 19, Code of Federal Regulations, Part
12.80 is enclosed, Enclosure 3.

Sincerely,

Francis Armstrong
Director
Office of Vehicle Safety Compliance
Enforcement

3 Enclosures

Aug-26-1983   Suspense Date: 17Oct83

                                 Port Code   : SFR-2801
                                 Date of Decl :   6-17-83   Letter Code: JG2
                                 Cus Entry No : 300798   Box No: 3

       (SPECIFIC ITEMS TO BE CONFORMED)

                                                              Effective
                                                              Date of
Make   Type   Model No   Serial No   FMVSS

PORSCHE   911SC   911661   0202   CAR:

Number   Description

101 CONTROL LOCATION, IDENTIFICATION, AND ILLUMINATION
102 TRANS. SHIFT LEVER SEQ., STARTER INTERLOCK, AND TRANS. BRAKING
103 WINDSHIELD DEFROSTING AND DEFOGGING SYSTEMS
104 WINDSHIELD WIPING AND WASHING SYSTEM
105 HYDRAULIC SERV. BRK., EMERGENCY BRK., AND PARKING BRK. SYSTEMS
106 BRAKE HOSES
107 REFLECTING SURFACES
108 LAMPS, REFLECTIVE DEVICES, AND ASSOCIATED EQUIPMENT
109 NEW PNEUMATIC TIRES
110 TIRE SELECTION AND RIMS
111 REARVIEW MIRRORS
112 HEADLAMP CONCEALMENT DEVICES
113 HOOD LATCH SYSTEMS
114 THEFT PROTECTION
115 VEHICLE IDENTIFICATION NUMBER
116 MOTOR VEHICLE BRAKE FLUIDS
118 POWER-OPERATED WINDOW SYSTEMS
124 ACCELERATOR CONTROL SYSTEMS
201 OCCUPANT PROTECTION IN INTERIOR IMPACT
202 HEAD RESTRAINTS
203 IMPACT PROTECTION FOR THE DRIVER FROM THE STEERING CONTROL SYSTEM
204 STEERING CONTROL REARWARD DISPLACEMENT
205 GLAZING MATERIALS
206 DOOR LOCK AND DOOR RETENTION COMPONENTS
207 SEATING SYSTEMS
208 OCCUPANT CRASH PROTECTION
209 SEAT BELT ASSEMBLIES
210 SEAT BELT ASSEMBLY ANCHORAGES
211 WHEEL NUTS, WHEEL DISCS, AND HUB CAPS
212 WINDSHIELD MOUNTING
214 SIDE DOOR STRENGTH
215 EXTERIOR PROTECTION
216 ROOF CRUSH RESISTANCE
301 FUEL SYSTEM INTEGRITY
302 FLAMMABILITY OF INTERIOR MATERIALS

GENERAL GUIDE FOR
SUBSTANTIATION OF COMPLIANCE WITH FMVSS 214 and 215
and 49 CFR 581

The statement of compliance must contain certain basic engineering data presented in a clear and conclusive manner and in sufficient detail to establish conformance with the given standard. While there may be various ways for presentation of the data, listed below are the minimum items of information that the statement must contain; in some cases more extensive information may be required than here shown. Standardization of your modifications and data presentation may further reduce the processing time of your statement by permitting, in established cases, a more cursory review of the information you furnish.

Information furnished for FMVSS 214 must cover the front and rear doors, as applicable, and that furnished for FMVSS 215 or 49 CFR 581, as applicable, must cover the front and rear bumper, and include corner impact data where applicable; data for 49 CFR 581 must include evidence of compliance with the dent and set, and damageability, criteria including performance under the application of a corner impact pendulum test, as applicable.

All analyses must contain full formulas and numerical calculations that were used in arriving at the respective conclusion that compliance is evident.

The information should be presented as follows ("x" shows applicability):

FMVSS 214 215	49 CFR 581	(FMVSS 215 in force from 9-72 through 8-78 = replaced by Part 581) (Part 581 in force effective 9-78)
x x	x	Vehicle Weight
x	x	Impact Velocity
x	x	Stroke of Energy Absorbing Device including force-vs-deflection curve
x	x	Kinetic Energy
x x	x	Maximum Force
x x	x	Maximum Bending Moment
x x	x	Distance to Outermost Fiber
x x	x	Moment of Inertia
x x	x	Section Modulus
x x	x	Maximum Stress
	x	Evidence of Meeting DENT and SET criteria
	x	Evidence of Meeting Vehicle Damageability Criteria under conditions of the pendulum and barrier impact tests.

Include layouts and detailed drawings, with dimensions and scale used, and clear photographs, showing the plan view, side view, and front view of the original frame, structural members, etc, that support the modifications, and the completed modifications.

List all materials in the overall design, showing strength specifications for each and identifying the source from which the specification is quoted. If the specifications are quoted from non-standard publications, foreign publications, vehicle or material manufacturer's information, etc, include copies of such information to positively document the specifications quoted; assumptions are not acceptable. If the required data, as outlined above, are not furnished, especially in reference to crash survivability requirements, this agency may require that the vehicle be exported from the United States.

You must furnish complete compliance data for each individual vehicle, except that identical vehicles covered by a given PCI-file or Customs entry may be covered by a single statement of compliance submitted for those vehicles relative to FMVSS 214 and 215, and/or 49 CFR 581 - Bumper Standard, as applicable, provided that the modifications that were performed on the vehicles are also identical and fully agree with details given in the statement of compliance. Reference to statements previously furnished for another PCI-file is of no consequence as each file must stand on its own documentation under review.

This information is furnished to assist you in correcting safety deficiencies that your vehicle may have, and guide you in your preparation of your compliance statement so that your bond may be released.

Please note that while your vehicle may have some of the required safety features, there are areas where compliance with the given Federal Motor Vehicle Safety Standards (FMVSS) is questionable. Unless you clearly substantiate conformity of your vehicle with all applicable FMVSS, including those questionable where modifications may not have been required, your statement may appear unclear and be rejected until you submit additional data. In such cases the bond release action is delayed due to additional correspondence involved.

To simplify the aspect of technical substantiation of your vehicle's compliance, we suggest that you use photographs showing the respective safety feature which you describe in the written part of your statement; this is in addition to the "Statement of Compliance", Form HS-189. Where photographs cannot be made or would be impractical to use, furnish a detailed description of the item so that there is no question of compliance and/or your understanding of the requirement. Examples of statements substantiating compliance are shown below and on the reverse side hereof. However, they are not all-inclusive and do not represent the requirements of all FMVSS that may apply to your vehicle.

Remember that:
   a. All items on the vouchers identify the FMVSS to which they apply otherwise it may be impossible to recognize them as pertinent to the issue.
   b. Photographs must be clear to be of value and identify the FMVSS features which are referenced in the written part of the statement of compliance.
   c. All individual pages, photographs, vouchers, sheets of paper, etc, must show the full and correct chassis serial number of the vehicle to which they apply to prevent loss or misplacement.
   d. Your statement of compliance must be signed and dated. If the importer of record, as shown on the Form HS-7 and the FMVSS printout, is a company, there must be enclosed a notarized statement (use of corporate seal is acceptable) by an recognized officer of the company designating a person authorized to sign the statement of compliance in behalf of the company. Statements bearing an unidentified signature will be rejected.
   e. While there may be requirements which, in your opinion, are unnecessary, there is no provision in the law under which anyone may be exempted from compliance.

Listed below are some of the FMVSS where compliance is questionable in vehicles which were not manufactured for the U.S. market. You should therefore describe how your vehicle meets these requirements even if modifications were not required, providing that the given FMVSS is applicable to your vehicle as shown on the printout already furnished to you. When filling out the Form HS-189, write "N/A" where the requirement is not applicable.

FMVSS
101 - Control identification by word/symbol
      Illumination of control identification
102 - Shift pattern on gearshift knob or elsewhere
105 - Dual circuit brake master cylinder
      Brake failure warning system, including warning lamp and means for testing it
108 - Sealed beam headlamps; parking lamps; sidemarker lamps and reflectors
110 - Tire information placard
111 - Outside mirror within reach of driver
114 - Steering lock; ignition key buzzer
115 - VIN plate on dashboard, nonremovable
202 - Head restraints (headrests)
203 - Impact-absorbing steering wheel
204 - Impact-absorbing steering column

FMVSS
205 - Windshield etched with marking "AS-1"
206 - Rear door locks without possibility to open door from inside with door handle when the lock button is down
207 - Front seat backrests with lock (2-door models only)
208 - Seat belts in front and rear; single-point pushbutton release; locking retractors; warning light and buzzer
211 - Racing-type wheel nuts with projecting wings
212 - Non-popout windshield (glued-in)
214 - Side door beams (in all dors)
215 - U.S.-type bumpers with additional buffers and cushions (9-72 to 8-73); with shockabsorbers, meeting the 5 mph impact requirement front and rear (9-73 to 8-78); non-damage bumpers, soft-surface, etc (from 9-78 on)
302 - Flammability of interior materials (may be ok if vinyl or leather, questionable if cloth)

(*)-Continued below-

EXAMPLES OF SUBSTANTIATING STATEMENTS

Shown below are several examples of statements which may aid you in formulating your own substantiation of compliance:

FMVSS 101 - ORIGINAL: Refer to photograph # __ showing that all controls subject to this FMVSS are properly identified.

         ORIGINAL: Refer to photograph # __ showing lamp fixtures which illuminate the control identification features subject to this FMVSS. Identification of the following controls is self-illuminated by light sources contained within the fixture itself: (list the controls)

         ORIGINAL: Intensity of control illumination is regulated by adjusting the headlamp switch knob.

         OR ---

-Continued on other side-

(*)

      Part 581 - Nonconforming bumpers front and rear

FMVSS 101 - MODIFIED: Refer to photograph # __ showing that all controls subject to this FMVSS are properly identified. The only modification required was the installation of a headlamp switch identification plate
listed on repair voucher # __, item # ___.

MODIFIED: Refer to photograph # __ showing lamps which illuminate the control identification features
subject to this FMVSS. The installed lamps are listed on repair voucher # __, item # __.

ORIGINAL: Intensity of control illumination is regulated by the headlamp switch knob (photograph # __).
No modifications were required to comply with this part of the standard.

FMVSS 105 - ORIGINAL: Refer to photograph # __ showing the dual brake master cylinder and connecting wires which
activate the brake failure warning lamp in the event of failure in the hydraulic brake system. The brake
failure warning lamp is located on the dashboard (photograph # ___) and its bulb can be tested by actua-
ting the parking brake lever. No modifications were required to meet the requirements of this FMVSS.

OR ---

FMVSS 105 - MODIFIED: Refer to photograph # __ showing the dual brake master cylinder and connecting wires which
activate the brake failure warning lamp in the even of failure in the hydraulic brake system (refer to
voucher # __, item # __, listing the required brake master cylinder). Refer to photograph # __ showing
the brake failure warning lamp as installed on the dashboard (refer to voucher # __, item # __, listing
the required lamp). The bulb in the brake failure lamp can be tested by depressing the lamp lens.
I performed the modification myself in accordance with instructions contained in the shop manual for
this vehicle.

FMVSS 110 - MODIFIED: Refer to photograph # __ showing the required placard as installed in the glove compartment
of the vehicle. I purchased the placard from my local dealer.

OR --

FMVSS 110 - MODIFIED: Refer to photograph # __ showing the required placard as installed in the glove compartment
of the vehicle. I made the placard myself. I calculated the vehicle capacity weight in the following
way:
    Manufacturer's specified maximum permissible gross vehicle weight .... 4,500 lbs
    Curb weight (car empty with full tank and otherwise road-ready) .... 3,670 lbs
    Vehicle capacity weight (payload) .... 830 lbs

FMVSS 212 - ORIGINAL: Refer to statement from the U.S. representative of the manufacturer of this car showing that
the windshield is installed in same way as in the U.S.-model of this car. (Statements from sources other
than the manufacturer of the vehicle or his U.S. representative are not acceptable because compliance
with FMVSS 212 cannot be determined without access to factory records.)

OR ---

FMVSS 212 - MODIFIED: Refer to voucher # __ showing installation of the windshield according to the vehicle manufacturer's specifications, including the use of U.S.-type windshield moulding and special retaining cement.

FMVSS 214 - ORIGINAL: Refer to photograph # __ showing the U.S.-model doors with the reinforcing side beams exposed
to view as installed in this vehicle, and copy of page # __ from the vehicle's spare parts manual showing
that identical doors are used by the manufacturer in both U.S. and non-U.S. versions of this vehicle.
OR ---

FMVSS 214 - MODIFIED: Refer to photograph # __ showing the modified doors with the reinforcing side beams exposed to
view as installed in this vehicle. Also refer to voucher # __, item # __, and to the enclosed engineering
analysis showing full formulas and numerical calculations that were used in designing the reinforcements
to meet the requirements of this FMVSS.

FMVSS 215 - MODIFIED: Refer to photographs # __ and # __ showing the modified front and rear bumpers, and a copy
of page # __ and page # __ from the vehicle's spare parts manual showing all components of U.S.-model
front and rear bumpers used to meet the requirements of this FMVSS and installed in this vehicle. The
bumpers now represent a copy of those used in the U.S.-model version of this vehicle.

OR ---

FMVSS 215 - MODIFIED: Refer to photographs # __ and # __ showing the modified front and rear bumpers, and to voucher
__, items # __, with enclosed engineering analysis showing full formulas and numerical calculations that
were used in designing the reinforced bumper system to meet the requirements of this FMVSS. Photographs
__ thru # __ further illsutrate the bumper and frame reinforcement features.

Federal Motor Vehicle Safety Standards and Procedures

For Customs Declaration and Certification of Imported Motor Vehicles

U.S. Department of Transportation

National Highway Traffic Safety Administration

DOT HS 805 674
REVISED APRIL 1985

FOREWORD

In September of 1966, the National Traffic and Motor Vehicle Safety Act was signed into law. This law directs the Secretary of Transportation to issue Federal motor vehicle safety standards to which motor vehicle manufacturers must conform. The first such standards became effective on all vehicles manufactured on or after January 1, 1968, for sale or use in the United States, with the exception of FMVSS No. 209, which was effective upon issuance on March 1, 1967.

Additional standards have been added each year, and still others are in the process of being developed and issued. In 1972, the Motor Vehicle Information and Cost Saving Act was enacted. This legislation directs the Secretary of Transportation to promulgate property loss reduction standards and odometer disclosure regulations. This booklet lists the Federal motor vehicle safety standards and odometer disclosure requirements issued as of March 1985, and provides a brief description of each.

Also outlined are some of the problems importers may encounter in the importation of motor vehicles whose conformance to the standards is not certified by the original manufacturer. It should be noted that statements herein apply only to the Federal Motor Vehicle Safety Standards. For information concerning exhaust emission control, importers should contact:

Environmental Protection Agency
Manufacturers Operations Division (EN-340)
Investigations/Imports Section
401 M Street, S.W.
Washington, D.C. 20460

SUMMARY DESCRIPTION OF STANDARDS*

STANDARD NO. 101 · Controls and Displays Passenger Cars (Effective 1-1-68)
Requires that essential controls be located within reach of the driver when the driver is restrained by a lap belt and upper torso restraint, and that certain controls mounted on the instrument panel be identified.

Passenger Cars (Effective 1-1-72), Multipurpose Passenger Vehicles, Trucks, and Buses (Effective 9-1-72)
All manually operated controls must be identified by words.

Passenger Cars, Multipurpose Passenger Vehicles, Trucks, and Buses (Effective 9-1-72)
Except for foot-operated controls or manually operated controls mounted on the steering column, the identification of essential controls and displays must be illuminated whenever the headlamps are lit.

Passenger Cars, Multipurpose Passenger Vehicles, Trucks, and Buses (Effective 9-1-80)
Certain essential hand-operated controls and certain displays must be identified by a symbol, and such identification be illuminated.

STANDARD NO. 102 · Transmission Shift Lever Sequence, Starter Interlock, and Transmission Braking Effect · Passenger Cars, Multipurpose Passenger Vehicles, Trucks, and Buses (Effective 1-1-68)
Requires that the automatic transmission shift lever sequences have the neutral position placed between forward and reverse drive positions. Its purpose is to reduce the likelihood of driver error in shifting. Also required is an interlock to prevent starting the vehicle in reverse and forward drive positions and an engine-braking effect in one of the lower gears at vehicle speeds below 25 miles per hour.

STANDARD NO. 103 · Windshield Defrosting and Defogging Systems · Passenger Cars, Multipurpose Passenger Vehicles, Trucks, and Buses (Effective 1-1-68)
Requires that all vehicles manufactured for sale in the continental United States be equipped with windshield defrosters and defogging systems. Test conditions are also specified for passenger cars.

STANDARD NO. 104 · Windshield Wiping and Washing Systems · Passenger Cars (Effective 1-1-68), Multipurpose Passenger Vehicles, Trucks, and Buses (Effective 1-1-69)
Specifies the windshield area to be wiped and requires high-performance washers with two or more speed power-driven systems. The wipers must be able to sweep the windshield at least 45 times a minute, regardless of engine load. Tables prescribing the minimum size of wiped areas have been added for passenger cars.

STANDARD NO. 105 · Hydraulic Brake System · Passenger Cars (Effective 1-1-68) and School Buses (Effective 4-1-77) Other Buses, Trucks and Multipurpose Passenger Vehicles (Effective 9-1-83)
Requires motor vehicles utilizing hydraulic brakes to have a split brake system, incorporating service and emergency features that are capable of stopping the vehicle under certain specified conditions, a parking brake system capable of holding light vehicles on a 30 percent grade and heavy vehicles on a 20 percent grade, and a warning light system to indicate loss of pressure or low fluid level, antilock system failure, and parking brake application.

STANDARD NO. 106 · Brake Hoses · Passenger Cars and Multipurpose Passenger Vehicles (Effective 1-1-68), Trucks, Buses, Trailers, Motorcycles, and Equipment (Effective 9-1-74)
The standard establishes performance and labeling requirements for hydraulic, air, and vacuum brake hoses, brake hose assemblies, and brake hose fittings for all motor vehicles.

STANDARD NO. 107 · Reflecting Surfaces · Passenger Cars, Multipurpose Passenger Vehicles, Trucks, and Buses (Effective 1-1-68)
The reflection of the sun into the driver's eyes from shiny surfaces has long been a safety hazard. This standard requires that windshield wiper arms, inside windshield moldings, horn rings, and frames and brackets of inside rearview mirrors have matte surfaces which will greatly reduce the likelihood of hazardous reflection into the driver's eyes.

*(Title 49 Code of Federal Regulations Part 571)

STANDARD NO. 108 · Lamps, Reflective Devices, and Associated Equipment · Passenger Cars, Multipurpose Passenger Vehicles, Trucks, Trailers, Buses, and Motorcycles (Effective 1-1-68 for vehicles 80 or more inches in width, effective 1-1-69 for all others)

This standard specifies requirements for lamps, reflective devices, and associated equipment for signaling and to enable safe operation in darkness and other conditions of reduced visibility. Side marker lights and reflectors, hazard warning and backup lights, and replacement equipment are included in the requirements for these vehicles.

STANDARD NO. 109 · New Pneumatic Tires · Passenger Cars (Effective 1-1-68)

Specifies tire dimensions and laboratory test requirements for bead unseating resistance; strength, endurance, and high-speed performance; defines tire load rating; and specifies labeling requirements.

STANDARD NO. 110 · Tire Selection and Rims · Passenger Cars (Effective 4-1-68)

Specifies requirements for original equipment tire and rim selection on new cars to prevent overloading. These include placard requirements relating to load distribution as well as rim performance requirements under conditions of tire deflation.

STANDARD NO. 111 · Rearview Mirrors · Passenger Cars, Multipurpose Passenger Vehicles (Effective 1-1-68), Trucks, Buses, and Motorcycles (Effective 2-26-77)

Specifies requirements for rearview mirrors to provide the driver with a clear and reasonably unobstructed view to the rear. On passenger cars it requires an outside rearview mirror on the driver's side, and when the inside mirror does not provide a sufficient field of view because of the size or location of the rear window, an additional outside mirror on the passenger side is required. Also, the inside mirror must be designed to reduce the likelihood of injury on impact. Trucks and buses must have mirrors on both sides.

STANDARD NO. 112 · Headlamp Concealment Devices · Passenger Cars, Multipurpose Passenger Vehicles, Trucks, Buses, and Motorcycles (Effective 1-1-69)

Specifies that any fully opened headlamp concealment device shall remain fully opened whether either or both of the following occur: (a) any loss of power to or within the device or (b) any malfunction of wiring or electrical supply for controlling the concealment device.

STANDARD NO. 113 · Hood Latch Systems · Passenger Cars, Multipurpose Passenger Vehicles, Trucks, and Buses (Effective 1-1-69)

Specifies requirements for a hood latch system for each hood. A front-opening hood which in any open position partially or completely obstructs a driver's forward view through the windshield must be provided with a second latch position on the hood latch system or with a second hood latch system.

STANDARD NO. 114 · Theft Protection · Passenger Cars (Effective 1-1-70) Multipurpose Passenger Vehicles, Trucks, and Buses (10,000 or less GVWR) (Effective 9-1-83)

This standard requires that each passenger car have a key-locking system that whenever the key is removed prevents normal activation of the car's engine and also prevents either steering or self-mobility of the car, or both.

STANDARD NO. 115 · Vehicle Identification Number, Passenger Cars (Effective 1-1-69), Multipurpose Passenger Vehicles, Trucks, Buses, Motorcycles and Trailers (Effective 9-1-80)

Specifies requirements for the content and format of a number to facilitate identification of a vehicle and must be permanently affixed to the vehicle.

STANDARD NO. 116 · Hydraulic Brake Fluids (Effective 1-1-68, Amended 3-1-72)

Requires minimum physical characteristics for three grades of brake fluids, DOT 3, DOT 4, and DOT 5, for use in hydraulic brake systems in all motor vehicles. Also establishes labeling requirements for brake fluid and hydraulic system mineral oil.

STANDARD NO. 117 · Retreaded Pneumatic Tires · Passenger Cars (Effective 1-1-72)

Prohibits certain practices in the manufacture of retreaded tires which might weaken the completed tire. Certain labeling information is also required.

STANDARD NO. 118 · Power-Operated Window Systems · Passenger Cars and Multipurpose Passenger Vehicles (Effective 2-1-71)

This standard specifies requirements to minimize the likelihood of death or injury from accidental operation of power-operated window systems. Requires that power-operated window systems be inoperable when ignition is in an off position or when key is removed.

STANDARD NO. 119 · New Pneumatic Tires · Multipurpose Passenger Vehicles, Trucks, Buses, Trailers, and Motorcycles (Effective 3-1-75)
Specifies strength, endurance, and high speed performance and marking requirements for new pneumatic tires manufactured for use on multipurpose passenger vehicles, trucks, trailers, buses, and motorcycles.

STANDARD NO. 120 · Tire Selection and Rims for Vehicles Other Than Passenger Cars (Effective 8-1-76)
This standard requires new vehicles to have tires conforming to Standard No. 119 or Standard No. 109 and rims designated in the tire association manuals as fitting them. It specifies marking requirements for rims and requires additional tire and rim size designations, pressure and speed restrictions, and weight rating information.

STANDARD NO. 121 · Air Brake Systems · Trucks, Buses (Effective 3-1-75), and Trailers (Effective 1-1-75)
Establishes performance and equipment requirements on vehicles equipped with air brake systems, for service, emergency, and parking brake capability.

STANDARD NO. 122 · Motorcycle Brake Systems · Motorcycles (Effective 1-1-74)
Establishes equipment and performance requirements on brake systems appropriate for two-wheeled and three-wheeled motorcycles. Each motorcycle is required to have either a split hydraulic service brake system or two independently actuated service brake systems.

STANDARD NO. 123 · Motorcycle Controls and Displays (Effective 9-1-74)
Specifies requirements for the location, operation, identification and illumination of motorcycle controls and displays and for stands and footrests.

STANDARD NO. 124 · Accelerator Control Systems · Passenger Cars, Multipurpose Passenger Vehicles, Trucks, and Buses (Effective 9-1-73)
Establishes requirements for the return of a vehicle's throttle to the idle position when the driver removes his or her foot from the accelerator control, or in the event of a breakage or disconnection in the accelerator control system.

STANDARD NO. 125 · Warning Devices (Effective 1-1-74)
Establishes shape, size, and performance requirements for reusable day and night warning devices that can be erected on or near the roadway to warn approaching motorists of the presence of a stopped vehicle. It applies only to devices that do not have self-contained energy sources.

STANDARD NO. 126 · Truck-Camper Loading (Effective 1-1-73)
Requires manufacturers of slide-in campers to affix a label to each camper that contains information relating to certification, identification, and proper loading and to provide more detailed loading information in the owner's manual.

STANDARD NO. 201 · Occupant Protection in Interior Impact · Passenger Cars (Effective 1-1-68), Multipurpose Passenger Vehicles, Trucks, and Buses (9-1-81) 10,000 lbs. or Less.
Over a wide range of impact speeds, injuries suffered by occupants are largely determined by how well the structures on the inside of the vehicle cushion the human body hitting them. This standard specifies requirements to afford impact protection for occupants. It contains requirements for padded instrument panels, seat backs, sun visors, armrests. Glove compartment doors are required to remain closed during a crash.

STANDARD NO. 202 · Head Restraints · Passenger Cars (Effective 1-1-69)
Specifies requirements for head restraints to reduce the frequency and severity of neck injuries in rear-end and other collisions.

STANDARD NO. 203 · Impact Protection for the Driver From the Steering Control System · Passenger Cars (Effective 1-1-68), Multipurpose Vehicles, Trucks, and Buses GVWR* of 10,000 lbs. or less (Effective 9-1-81)
Specifies requirements for minimizing chest, neck, and facial injuries by providing steering systems that yield forward, cushioning the impact of the driver's chest by absorbing much of his or her impact energy in front-end crashes. Such systems are highly effective in reducing the likelihood of serious and fatal injuries.

* GVWR gross vehicle weight rating.

STANDARD NO. 204 - Steering Control Rearward Displacement - Passenger Cars (Effective 1-1-68), Multipurpose Passenger Vehicles, Trucks, and Buses with Unloaded Vehicle Weight of 4,000 Pounds or Less (9-1-81)

Specifies requirements limiting the rearward displacement of the steering column into the passenger compartment to reduce the likelihood of chest, neck, or head injuries.

STANDARD NO. 205 - Glazing Materials - Passenger Cars, Multipurpose Passenger Vehicles, Motorcycles, Trucks and Buses (Effective 1-1-68)

Specifies requirements for all glazing materials used in windshields, windows, and interior partitions of motor vehicles. Its purpose is to reduce the likelihood of lacerations and to minimize the possibility of occupants penetrating the windshield in collisions.

STANDARD NO. 206 - Door Locks and Door Retention Components - Passenger Cars (Effective 1-1-68), Multipurpose Passenger Vehicles (Effective 1-1-70), and Trucks (Effective 1-1-72)

Requires locking systems and specifies load requirements for door latches and door hinge systems to minimize the probability of occupants being thrown from the vehicle as a result of forces encountered in vehicle impact.

STANDARD NO. 207 - Seating Systems - Passenger Cars (Effective 1-1-68), Multipurpose Passenger Vehicles, Trucks, and Buses (Effective 1-1-72)

Establishes requirements for seats, their attachment assemblies, and their installation, to minimize the possibility of failure as a result of forces acting on the seat in vehicle impact.

STANDARD NO. 208 - Occupant Crash Protection (Effective 3-10-71)

This standard specifies requirements for both active and passive occupant crash protection systems for passenger cars, multipurpose passenger vehicles, trucks, and the driver's seat in buses. Generally, the following options are permitted:

Passenger Cars (Effective 1-1-68)

Lap or lap and shoulder seat belt assemblies in each designated seating position; except in convertibles, lap and shoulder seat belts are required in each front outboard seating position.

Passenger Cars (Effective 1-1-72)

a. A complete passive protection system, or
b. Lap belts with belt warning and meeting certain crash protection requirements specified for a 30-mph frontal barrier crash, or
c. In each designated seating position a lap or lap and shoulder seat belt assembly with seat belt warning; seat belt assemblies in outboard designated seating positions must have a single-point pushbutton release and emergency-locking or automatic-locking seat belt retractors.

Passenger Cars (Effective 9-1-73)

Same requirements as for passenger cars effective 1-1-72 except that the upper torso restraints must adjust by means of an emergency-locking retractor.

Buses (Effective 1-1-72)

The bus driver's seat must be equipped as follows:
a. A complete passive protection system or
b. A lap or lap and shoulder seat belt assembly.

Multipurpose Passenger Vehicles and Trucks (Effective 1-1-72)

Certain multipurpose passenger vehicles and trucks must meet option "a" or option "b" specified for passenger cars, above.

STANDARD NO. 209 - Seat Belt Assemblies - Passenger Cars, Multipurpose Passenger Vehicles, Trucks, and Buses (Effective 3-1-67)

Specifies requirements for seat belt assemblies. The requirements apply to straps, webbing, or similar material, as well as to all necessary buckles and other fasteners and all hardware designed for installing the assembly in a motor vehicle, and to the installation, usage, and maintenance instructions for the assembly.

STANDARD NO. 210 - Seat Belt Assembly Anchorages - Passenger Cars (Effective 1-1-68), Multipurpose Passenger Vehicles Trucks, and Buses (Effective 7-1-71)

Specifies the requirements for seat belt assembly anchorages to ensure effective occupant restraint and to reduce the likelihood of failure in collisions.

STANDARD NO. 211 - Wheel Nuts, Wheel Discs, and Hub Caps - Passenger Cars and Multipurpose Passenger Vehicles and Equipment (Effective 1-1-68)

Requires that "spinner" hub caps and other winged projections (both functional and nonfunctional) be removed from wheel nuts, wheel discs, and hub caps. Its purpose is to eliminate a potential hazard to pedestrians and cyclists.

STANDARD NO. 212 · Windshield Mounting · Passenger Cars (Effective 1-1-70), Multipurpose Passenger Vehicles, Trucks, and Buses 10,000 lbs. or Less (9-1-78)

This standard requires that, when tested as described, each windshield mounting must be anchored in place and retain one of two specified percentages of its periphery in a crash situation. The purpose of the standard is to keep vehicle occupants within the confines of the passenger compartment during a crash.

STANDARD NO. 213 · Child Seating Systems (Effective 4-1-71, amended 1-1-81)

Specifies requirements for dynamic testing of child seating systems to minimize the likelihood of injury and/or death to children in vehicle crashes or sudden stops. Includes requirements for providing information for proper installation and use.

STANDARD NO. 214 · Side Door Strength · Passenger Cars (Effective 1-1-73)

This standard specifies requirements for crush resistance levels in side doors of passenger cars to minimize the safety hazard caused by intrusion into the passenger compartment in a side impact accident.

STANDARD NO. 215 · Passenger Cars (Effective 9-1-72)

(Superseded by PART 581 on 9-1-78)

STANDARD NO. 216 · Roof Crush Resistance · Passenger Cars (Effective 9-1-73)

Sets minimum strength requirements for passenger car roofs to reduce the likelihood of roof collapse in a rollover accident. The standard provides an alternative to conformity with the rollover tests of Standard No. 208.

STANDARD NO. 217 · Bus Window Retention and Release · Buses (Effective 9-1-73)

This standard establishes minimum requirements for bus window retention and release to reduce the likelihood of passenger ejection in accidents; and for emergency exits to facilitate passenger exit in emergencies. It also requires that each school bus have an interlock system which will prevent the engine from starting if an emergency door is unlocked and an audible warning system which will sound an alarm if an emergency door release mechanism is not closed while the engine is running.

STANDARD NO. 218 · Motorcycle Helmets (Effective 3-1-74)

Requires most helmets manufactured for use by motorcyclists and other motor vehicle users to meet minimum specified performance requirements. It establishes test requirements for impact attenuation, penetration, and retention, and criteria for peripheral vision clearance, harmful projections, and labeling.

STANDARD NO. 219 · Windshield Zone Intrusion · Passenger Cars (Effective 9-1-76), Multipurpose Passenger Vehicles, Trailers, Buses of 10,000 lbs. or Less Gross Vehicle Weight Rating (Effective 9-1-77) 5,500 lbs. Unloaded Weight (Effective 4-3-80)

The purpose of this standard is to reduce crash injuries and fatalities that result from occupants contacting vehicle components displaced near or through the windshield. The standard regulates the intrusion of vehicle parts from outside the occupant compartment into a defined zone in front of the windshield during a frontal barrier crash test.

STANDARD NO. 220 · School Bus Rollover Protection · School Buses (Effective 4-1-77)

This standard specifies minimum strength requirements for school bus roofs to reduce the likelihood of roof collapse in a rollover accident, and requires that emergency exits (except roof exits) be operable after the roof is subjected to forces that can be encountered in rollovers.

STANDARD NO. 221 · School Bus Body Joint Strength · School Buses (Effective 4-1-77)

This standard specifies minimum strength requirements for body panel joints to improve the structural integrity of the passenger compartment and to reduce the likelihood of lacerative injuries to occupants caused by the sharp edges of body panels that tear loose in crashes.

STANDARD NO. 222 · School Bus Passenger Seating · Crash Protection · School Buses (Effective 4-1-77)

This standard specifies seating, restraining barrier, and impact zone requirements for school buses. The standard relies on compartmentalization between well-padded and well-constructed seats to provide occupant protection on school buses.

STANDARD NO. 301 - Fuel System Integrity - Passenger Cars (Effective 1-1-68), Multipurpose Passenger Vehicles, Trucks, and Buses under 10,000 lbs. (Effective 9-1-76), and School Buses Over 10,000 lbs. (Effective 4-1-77)

This standard specifies requirements for the integrity and security of the entire fuel system, including the fuel tanks, fuel pump, carburetor, emission controls, lines, and connections in severe front, rear, or lateral barrier impact crash tests. Manufacturers must also be able to demonstrate that fuel loss will not exceed one ounce per minute in a static rollover test following these barrier crash tests, as well as not exceeding these limits after, and incidental to, the crash tests.

STANDARD NO. 302 - Flammability of Interior Materials - Passenger Cars, Multipurpose Passenger Vehicles, Trucks, and Buses (Effective 9-1-72)

This standard specifies burn resistance requirements for materials used in the occupant compartment of motor vehicles in order to reduce deaths and injuries caused by vehicle fires.

SUMMARY DESCRIPTION
OF OTHER REGULATIONS

PART 555 · Temporary Exemptions From Motor Vehicle Safety Standards (Effective 1-29-73)

This regulation provides a means by which manufacturers of motor vehicles may obtain temporary exemptions from specific safety standards on the grounds of substantial economic hardship, facilitation of the development of new motor vehicle safety or low-emission engine features, or existence of an equivalent overall level of motor vehicle safety.

PART 557 · Petitions for Hearings on Notification and Remedy of Defects (Effective 1-31-77)

This regulation establishes procedures for the submission and disposition of petitions for hearings on whether a manufacturer has reasonably met his or her obligation to notify owners, purchasers, and dealers of a safety-related defect or failure to comply with a safety standard or to remedy such defect or noncompliance. This part also establishes procedures for holding such a hearing, effective January 31, 1977.

PART 566 · Manufacturer Identification (Effective 2-1-72)

Requires manufacturers of motor vehicles and motor vehicle equipment (except tires) to which a motor vehicle safety standard applies to submit identifying information and descriptions of the items they produce to the Department of Transportation. Revised information is also required when necessary to keep the entry current.

PART 567 · Certification Regulation (Effective 8-31-69)

This part specifies the content and location of and other requirements for the label or tag to be affixed to motor vehicles and motor vehicle equipment manufactured after August 31, 1969. This certificate will provide the consumer with information to assist him or her in determining which of the Federal Motor Vehicle Safety Standards are applicable to the vehicle or equipment, and its date of manufacture. An amendment effective Jan. 1, 1972 requires Gross Vehicle Weight Information on the Certification label.

PART 568 · Vehicles Manufactured in Two or More Stages (Effective 1-1-72)

This part requires the furnishing of information relative to a vehicle's conformity to motor vehicle safety standards. It requires manufacturers of incomplete vehicles to list each standard applicable to the types of vehicles into which the incomplete vehicle may be manufactured that is in effect at the time of manufacture of the incomplete vehicle.

PART 569 · Regrooved Tires · Applies to All Motor Vehicle Regrooved or Regroovable Tires Manufactured or Regrooved After April 1, 1969

The regulation allows only tires designed for the regrooving process to be regrooved; specifies dimensional and conditional requirements for the tire after the regrooving process; and sets forth labeling requirements for the tire which is to be regrooved.

PART 570 · Vehicle In Use Inspection Standards (Effective 9-28-73)

Specifies procedures for the inspection of hydraulic service brake systems, steering and suspension systems, and tire and wheel assemblies of motor vehicles in use. It is intended to be implemented by the States with respect to the inspection of motor vehicles with gross vehicle weight ratings of 10,000 lbs. or less, except motorcycles and trailers.

PART 572 · Anthropomorphic Test Dummy (Effective 8-1-73)

This regulation describes the 50th percentile male anthropomorphic test dummy that is to be used for testing of motor vehicles for compliance with motor vehicle safety standards. The design and performance criteria specified are intended to describe a measuring tool with sufficient precision to give repetitive and correlative results under similar test conditions and to reflect adequately the protective performance of a vehicle with respect to human occupants. It is designed to be referenced by and become a part of the test procedures specified in motor vehicle safety standards such as Standard No. 208, Occupant Crash Protection.

PART 573 · Defect Reports (Effective 10-1-71)

This part specifies manufacturer requirements for reporting safety-related defects to the National Highway Traffic Safety Administration; for providing quarterly reports on defect notification campaigns; for providing copies of communications with dealers and purchasers concerning defects; and for maintaining owner lists.

PART 574 · Tire Identification and Record Keeping (Effective 5-22-71)

Applies to manufacturers, brand name owners, retreaders, and distributors and dealers of new and retread tires for use on motor vehicles, and to manufacturers and dealers of motor vehicles. Requires tire identification, and recording and reporting of names of tire purchasers.

PART 575 · Consumer Information Regulation (Effective 1-1-70)

Requires manufacturers to provide the following information to first purchasers:

Vehicle stopping distance. Manufacturers of passenger cars and motorcycles must provide information on stopping distance at specified speeds and under various conditions.

Truck-camper loading. Manufacturers of trucks that are capable of accommodating slide-in campers manufactured after April 1, 1973 must provide a cargo weight rating and the longitudinal limits within which the center of gravity for the cargo weight rating should be located.

Uniform Tire Quality Grading Standards. Manufacturers of passenger car tires must provide information on tread life, traction, and temperature resistance. The grades are displayed on the sidewall of the tire, on a label, and in a leaflet available at the tire dealer's store. All tires manufactured after April 1, 1980 are graded.

PART 577 · Defect and Noncompliance Notification (Effective 3-26-73)

Establishes requirements for the format and contents of manufacturer notification to the person who is the registered owner or to first purchasers of motor vehicles and motor vehicle equipment of a defect relating to motor vehicle safety or a noncompliance with a Federal motor vehicle safety standard.

PART 579 · Defect and Noncompliance Responsibility (Effective 9-30-78)

This regulation allocates between motor vehicle and equipment manufacturers the responsibilities under the 1974 Motor Vehicle and School Bus Safety Amendments for recalling and remedying defective motor vehicles and equipment or motor vehicles and equipment not built in compliance with the law.

PART 580 · Odometer Disclosure Requirements (Effective 3-1-73)

The regulation requires a person who transfers ownership of a motor vehicle to give the transferee a written disclosure of the mileage the vehicle has traveled.

PART 581 · Bumper Standard · Limited Damage (Effective 9-1-78); No Damage (Effective 9-1-79)

This standard specifies limitations on damage to non-safety-related components and vehicle surface areas. It also incorporates the requirements previously contained in Safety Standard No. 215.

Vehicles manufactured after September 1, 1978 must also be certified as conforming to the bumper standard required by the Cost Savings Act. This requirement has been incorporated into 49 CFR 567.

PROCEDURES FOR CUSTOMS DECLARATION AND CERTIFICATION OF IMPORTED MOTOR VEHICLES

AS TO CONFORMANCE WITH FEDERAL MOTOR VEHICLE SAFETY STANDARDS

Section No. 108 of the National Traffic and Motor Vehicle Safety Act of 1966 (the Act) specifies that all imported motor vehicles, new or used, manufactured on or after January 1, 1968 must conform to applicable Federal Motor Vehicle Safety Standards in effect on their date of manufacture.

The best evidence of conformity is the original manufacturer's certification label required by Section No. 114 of the Act as implemented by 49 CFR 567. Note should be taken that a certification label affixed to a vehicle manufactured on or after September 1, 1969 must show the date of manufacture and the vehicle identification number (VIN). The format of a typical passenger car label is illustrated below.

```
         MANUFACTURED BY
       THE FINE CAR CO., INC.
   ___________________________

          SEPTEMBER 1978
   ___________________________

    *  GVWR  0000
   **  GAWR  FRONT  0000
             REAR   0000
   ___________________________

   THIS VEHICLE CONFORMS TO ALL
   APPLICABLE FEDERAL MOTOR VEHICLE
   SAFETY AND BUMPER STANDARDS IN
   EFFECT ON THE DATE OF MANUFACTURE
   SHOWN ABOVE.
   ___________________________

   VEHICLE IDENTIFICATION
   NUMBER 0000
   TYPE
   PASSENGER CAR
```

    * Gross Vehicle Weight Rating
   ** Gross Axle Weight Rating

Customs regulation 19 CFR 12.80 was jointly issued by the Secretary of the Treasury and the Secretary of Transportation to provide procedural guidance and regulation for the importation of motor vehicles and items of motor vehicle equipment subject to the requirements of the Act.

In cases where the motor vehicle, whether imported for personal use or for resale, does not have affixed the certification label of the original manufacturer, the above regulation [19 CFR 12.80 (b) (1)] provides for eight alternative declarations which may be made by the importer on a Department of Transportation Form HS–7:

I Declare . . .

1. The vehicle or equipment item was manufactured on a date when no applicable safety standards were in effect.

2. The vehicle or equipment item conforms to all applicable safety standards (or, the vehicle does not conform solely because readily attachable equipment items, which will be attached to the vehicle before it is offered for sale to the first purchaser for purposes other than resale, are not attached) *and bears a certification label* or tag to that effect permanently affixed by the original manufacturer to the vehicle, to the equipment item, or to the outside of the container in which the equipment item is delivered, in accordance with regulations issued by the Secretary of Transportation (49 CFR Parts 555, 567, 568, and 571) under section 114 of the Act (15 U.S.C. 1403).

3. The vehicle or equipment item was not manufactured in conformity with all applicable safety standards, but it has been or will be brought into conformity. Within 120 days after entry, or within a period not to exceed 180 days after entry, if additional time is granted by the Administrator, National Highway Traffic Safety Administration ("Administrator, NHTSA"), the importer or consignee will submit a true and complete statement to the Administrator, NHTSA, identifying the manufacturer, contractor, or other person who has brought the vehicle or equipment item into conformity, describing the exact nature and extent of the work performed, and certifying that the vehicle or equipment item has been brought into conformity, and that the vehicle or equipment item

will not be sold or offered for sale until the Administrator, NHTSA, issues an approval letter to the district director stating that the conditions of the bond required by paragraph (e)(1) of this section have been satisfied.

4. The vehicle or equipment item is intended solely for export, and the vehicle or equipment item, and the outside of the container of the equipment item, if any, bears a label or tag to that effect.

5. The importer or consignee is a nonresident of the United States, is importing the vehicle or equipment item primarily for personal use for a period not exceeding 1 year from the date of entry, will not sell it in the United States during that period, and has stated his or her passport number and country of issue, if he or her has a passport, on the declaration.

6. The importer or consignee is a member of the armed forces of a foreign country on assignment in the United States; a member of the Secretariat of a public international organization so designated under the International Organizations Immunities Act (22 U.S.C. 288), as listed in 19 CFR 148.87, on assignment in the United States; or a member of the personnel of a foreign government on assignment in the United States who is within the class of persons for whom free entry of vehicles has been authorized by the Department of State; is importing the vehicle or equipment item for purposes other than resale; and has attached a copy of his or her official orders, if any, to the declaration (or, if a qualifying member of the personnel of a foreign government on assignment in the United States, the name of the embassy to which he or she is accredited is stated on the declaration).

7. The vehicle or equipment item is imported solely for the purpose of show, test, experiment, competition (a vehicle the configuration of which at the time of entry is such that it cannot be licensed for use on the public roads is considered to be imported for the purpose of competition), repair, or alteration, and the statement required by 19 CFR 12.80(c)(2) or (c)(3) is attached to the declaration.

8. The vehicle was not manufactured primarily for use on the public roads and is not a "motor vehicle" as defined in section 102 of the Act (15 U.S.C. 1391).

9. The vehicle is an "incomplete vehicle" as defined in 49 CFR Part 568.

In a large percentage of the importations under the authority of 19 CFR 12.80 (b)(1), one of the first three declarations above will apply. In the case of No. 1, the importer should be prepared to present documentary evidence to substantiate his or her declaration.

Declarations made under provisions of No. 3, above, in all probability pose the most difficulty for the importer. Note should be taken that this declaration—requiring posting of bond—covers entries wherein modifications have been accomplished prior to entry or are to be accomplished after entry. The National Highway Traffic Safety Administration is not in a position to advise as to the modifications necessary to bring any particular vehicle into conformance. The original manufacturer is best qualified to do this. The importer is advised to obtain specific information on the modifications necessary to bring the vehicle into conformity before entering into contractual arrangements for purchase. As a word of caution, it is pointed out that certain modifications may require extensive engineering, or be impractical or impossible, or the labor and/or material cost may be unduly expensive. This is particularly true of 1973 and later model vehicles.

Another prevalent difficulty encountered by importers making declarations under No. 3 above is connected with obtaining bond and producing the statements required by 19 CFR 12.80(e). This bond—to assure production of a conformity statement—must be in an amount equal to the value of the motor vehicle, as set forth in the entry, plus the estimated duty and other taxes connected with the importation. Individuals not having normal trade relations with customs house brokers or other bonding agencies acceptable to the U.S. Customs Service are cautioned to make bonding arrangements prior to shipment of motor vehicles from foreign ports in order to avoid unnecessary embarrassment or delay at the port of entry, as the motor vehicle cannot be admitted until bond is posted. The statement under declaration No. 3, required to be furnished within 120 days of entry, must describe the exact nature and extent of the work performed and identify the person making the modifications.

If the original manufacturer has not certified the specific individual vehicle you have or intend to purchase, the importer will bear the total responsibility for making the required modifications and for submitting, within 120 days of the date of entry into the United States, data to substantiate conformance with all standards applicable to the specific vehicle. The data must identify the manufacturer, contractor, or other person who has brought the vehicle into conformity and must describe in exact detail the nature and extent of the work performed. This you may find expensive and most difficult, if indeed at all possible, to accomplish. We strongly advise against the importation of a vehicle which is not certified by the manufacturer for sale on the American market. This is especially true of 1973 and later-model years. Failure to substantiate that the vehicle has been brought into conformity renders the importer liable for imposition of a civil penalty of up to $1,000 and/or assessment of liquidated damages in the amount of the value of the vehicle pursuant to the bond required by 19 CFR 12.80(e).

You are hereby advised that for some requirements dealing with crash survivability, specifically standards numbers 203, 204, 207, 210, 214, 216, 219, and 301, proof of conformance is difficult to achieve without the manufacturer's compliance statement, and in the event that the importer is unable to substantiate conformance, the Agency will press for redelivery and export of the vehicle.

In summary, your best assurance of being able to import your motor vehicle without difficulty is to obtain one built for the U.S. market and bearing the certification label of the original manufacturer.

Instructions from DOT give an idea of the things to be done. The instructions, however, do not tell important details. For instance, conformation may be done by a local shop, auto mechanic, or EPA-certified test centers. These businesses will usually handle all conversions and/or EPA testing for you; all you need to do is to bring the auto to them. Some only handle the DOT requirements, while others handle only the EPA requirements, and some do both. Usually, those shops that handle the DOT conformation will also prepare the detailed document package and submit it along with your DOT papers.

Costs vary according to the auto make and what has to be done as prescribed by DOT. In some cases names of these shops can be obtained from the local US customs agent or by writing to the Automobile Importers Compliance Association (AICA), 1607 New Hampshire Ave. N.W., Washington, DC 20009. Neither US customs nor I recommend any one shop or service.

The following check list should assist you in preparing the correct photos of the work being done for submission with your package. Remember to properly reference each photo with the correct FMVSS.

Many of the items called for may not be visible in your photos. Thus, it is important that an owners manual be included with your package. If you have the owners manual you should plan on providing a copy of it with the US owners manual in order to show the differences or lack of difference between the two cars.

Conforming your newly imported auto to DOT requirements is perhaps the most difficult aspect of the importation process. Considering that you have taken advantage of the one-time exemption from EPA requirements by bringing the auto in under your social security number, and that you are able to register it in your state, your only major hurdle is to conform the auto.

In California, registration can only be completed *after* both EPA and DOT requirements have been met.

Conformation takes time, especially if you do it yourself. Parts may be difficult to procure or nonexistent. If you work regular hours, time to get parts and put them on may be a problem. You may find that you are running out of time (120 days allocated by DOT) to do the work. Thus, it is important to begin work as soon as you get the auto from customs. Furthermore, the documentation package that the DOT requires takes even more time to prepare and is quite extensive.

Photo checklist for Dept. of Transportation FMVSS Modifications

AUTO _________________ CHASSIS # _________________

FMVSS 101
_______ 1. Headlight switch label
_______ 2. Hazard warning signal control
_______ 3. Windshield defogging controls
_______ 4. Heating and airconditioning controls
_______ 5. MPH Speedometer (after 8-31-80)

FMVSS 102
_______ 6. Shift selection pattern

FMVSS 104
_______ 7. Windshield washer water tank

FMVSS 105
_______ 8. Dual brake master cylinder (show brake lines & electric signal terminals)
_______ 9. Brake label on instrument cluster

FMVSS 107
_______ 10. Windshield wiper blades (dull finish)
_______ 11. Inside windshield moldings (dull finish)
_______ 12. Steering wheel (dull finish)
_______ 13. Inside rear view mirror frame and mounting bracket (dull finish)

FMVSS 108
_______ 14. Close-up of headlights (showing markings)
_______ 15. Full left side view of auto (showing side lights)
_______ 16. Full right side view of auto (showing side lights)
_______ 17. Full front view showing headlights
_______ 18. Rear view
_______ 19. License plate lights
_______ 20. Close-up of all four side lights (showing Class A reflector)

FMVSS 110
_______ 21. Vehicle capacity/tire pressure label attached to left front door jamb

FMVSS 113
_______ 22. Secondary safety hood latch

FMVSS 114
_______ 23. Warning Buzzer system (before installation)
_______ 24. Warning Buzzer system (after installation)

FMVSS 115
_______ 25. VIN plate

FMVSS 124
_______ 26. Throttle return spring (for autos 9-73 and newer)

FMVSS 202
_______ 27. Headrests

FMVSS 205
_______ 28. Windshield label
_______ 29. Side window label
_______ 30. Rear window label

FMVSS 206 (4 door autos only)
_______ 31. Rear door latches (new US version) (Hold up old latches along side to emphasize change over)

FMVSS 207 (2 door car only)
_______ 32. Control for releasing seat backs

FMVSS 208
_______ 33. Seatbelts (front)
_______ 34. Seatbelts (rear-when applicable)
_______ 35. Seatbelt label (front)
_______ 36. Seatbelt label (rear)
_______ 37. Seatbelt label (rear center)
_______ 38. Fasten seatbelt label (instrument panel)

FMVSS 212 (For autos 1979 and older)
When windshield is sealed in place by conversion company, show a photo of procedure and of seal tube (DOT approved urethane) or include invoice from professional glass shop

FMVSS 214
_______ 39. Door beams (along outside of each door—2-4 photos)
_______ 40. Door beams (inside doors and mounted, 2-4 photos)
_______ 41. Each mounting point of all door beams (4-8 photos)

FMVSS 215
_______ 42. Bumper guards added to bumper or structural support added behind bumper or original mountings of bumper when legal, such as Porsche 911 SC. (May require more than 1 photo)

FMVSS 301 (Fuel tank vent modification)
_______ 43. New vent line
_______ 44. One-way pressure valve

FMVSS 212 For autos 1979 and older
When windshield is sealed in place by conversion company, show a photo of procedure and of seal tube (DOT approved urethane) or include invoice from professional glass shop

Keep in mind that some items on this list may be combined in one photo even though they may be for different FMVSS. Reference can then be made when the photo list is assembled. Each photo should show auto's VIN (chassis number) on a card.

The following Compliance Data Evaluation Sheet is included here to show you what evaluation the DOT goes through when it receives your package. Studying this document should also indicate to you the various areas that need to be conformed, and what the DOT looks for in the work. Some of these may seem applicable and others do not apply. DOT may send you one of these if your documentation package is not complete.

COMPLIANCE DATA EVALUATION SHEET

Date ________________________

Importer ___________________________________   PCI # ___________________________

Make ___________________________________   VIN ___________________________

CE#/Date ___________________________________   FMVSS Date __________   Veh. Type __________

Review of compliance data on file for the referenced vehicle revealed insufficient documentation to establish conformance with the Federal Motor Vehicle Safety Standards (FMVSS) checked below:

FMVSS		FMVSS		FMVSS	
101---CONTROL LOCATION, IDENTIFICATION, AND ILLUMINATION		**113---HOOD LATCH SYSTEMS**		**210 ● SEAT BELT ASSEMBLY ANCHORAGES**	
( )	Controls and/or internal displays not identified with required words and/or symbols.	( )	No secondary hood retaining system.	( )	____ anchorages missing / nonconforming.
( )	Control and/or internal display identification not illuminated.	**114---THEFT PROTECTION**		**211 - WHEEL NUTS, WHEEL DISCS, AND HUB CAPS**	
( )	Control ID illumination not variable.	( )	No steering lock.	( )	Wheel nuts with winged projections.
102---TRANSMISSION SHIFT LEVER SEQUENCE, STARTER INTERLOCK, AND TRANSMISSION BRAKING EFFECT		( )	Key removable with lock unlocked.	**212 - WINDSHIELD MOUNTING**	
( )	No shift pattern in view of driver.	( )	No key warning system.	( )	Windshield not in conforming moulding.
103---WINDSHIELD DEFROSTING AND DEFOGGING SYSTEMS		**115---VEHICLE IDENTIFICATION NUMBER (VIN)**		( )	Windshield not in retention adhesive.
( )	No defroster in vehicle.	( )	No VIN plate readable from outside veh.	**214 ● SIDE DOOR STRENGTH**	
104---WINDSHIELD WIPING AND WASHING SYSTEMS		( )	VIN plate not permanently affixed.	( )	Door beams not installed in all doors.
( )	No two-speed windshield wiper system.	**118---POWER-OPERATED WINDOW SYSTEMS**		( )	Nonconforming door beam modification.
105---HYDRAULIC BRAKE SYSTEM		( )	Non-U.S. model configuration.	**215 - EXTERIOR PROTECTION (9-72 thru 8-78)**	
( )	No dual-circuit brake master cylinder.	**119---NEW PNEUMATIC TIRES FOR VEHICLES OTHER THAN PASS. CARS (Other than retreads)**		( )	Bumpers not modified.
( )	No brake failure warning system.	( )	Tires without valid ID number.	( )	Nonconforming bumper modification.
( )	Hydraulic brake fluid reservoir without informatory inscription.	( )	Tires without DOT symbol.	**216 ● ROOF CRUSH RESISTANCE**	
106---BRAKE HOSES		**120---TIRE SELECTION AND RIMS FOR MOTOR VEHICLES OTHER THAN PASSENGER CARS**		( )	No backup for non-U.S. body design.
( )	No required markings.	( )	Rims without DOT symbol.	**219 ● WINDSHIELD ZONE INTRUSION**	
107---REFLECTING SURFACES		( )	No tire/rim choice information label.	( )	No backup for non-U.S. body design.
( )	Bright chrome wiper arms & blades, horn ring, inside rearview mirror bracket.	**121---AIR BRAKE SYSTEMS**		**301 ● FUEL SYSTEM INTEGRITY**	
108---LAMPS, REFLECTIVE DEVICES, AND ASSOCIATED EQUIPMENT		( )	Non-U.S. model air brake system.	( )	No backup for non-U.S. body design.
( )	Nonconforming headlamps.	**122---MOTORCYCLE BRAKE SYSTEMS**		**302 - FLAMMABILITY OF INTERIOR MATERIALS**	
( )	Nonconforming headlamp housings.	( )	Non-U.S. model brake system.	( )	No backup for non-U.S. interior mat.
( )	No parking lamps.	**123---MOTORCYCLE CONTROLS AND DISPLAYS**		**PART 581 - BUMPER STANDARD (From 9-78 on)**	
( )	Parking lights not on with headlamps.	( )	Non-U.S. model controls and displays.	( )	Bumpers not modified.
( )	No sidemarker reflectors or lights.	**124---ACCELERATOR CONTROL SYSTEMS**		( )	Nonconforming bumper modification.
( )	Sidemarkers of improper color.	( )	Non-U.S. model accelerator controls.	**PART 567 - CERTIFICATION**	
( )	No hazard warning system.	**201---OCCUPANT PROTECTION IN INTERIOR IMPACT**		( )	No sample of actual label furnished.
( )	No turn signal lights.	( )	Instrument panel not energy-absorbing.	( )	Label removable without destruction.
109---NEW PNEUMATIC TIRES (Tires other than retreads, for passenger cars only)		**202---HEAD RESTRAINTS**		( )	Lettering not of proper contrast.
( )	Tires without DOT symbol.	( )	No head restraints.	( )	Vehicle manufacturer's name incorrect.
110---TIRE SELECTION AND RIMS		( )	Non-U.S. model head restraints.	( )	Mo/Yr of manufacture incorrect.
( )	No tire information placard.	**203 ● IMPACT PROTECTION FOR THE DRIVER FROM STEERING CONTROL SYSTEM**		( )	Weight ratings incorrect.
( )	Placard with incorrect data.	( )	Steering wheel not energy-absorbing.	( )	Improper format and order of data.
111---REARVIEW MIRRORS		**204 ● STEERING CONTROL REARWARD DISPLACEMENT**		( )	Bumper certification not in text.
( )	Required mirrors not of unit magnification: L/H ( ), R/H ( ), inside ( ).	( )	Steering column not energy-absorbing.		
( )	Outside mirror without driver's reach.	**205---GLAZING MATERIALS**			
112---HEADLAMP CONCEALMENT DEVICES		( )	Windshield not marked AS-1.		
( )	Non-U.S. model configuration.	**206---DOOR LOCK & DOOR RETENTION COMPONENTS**			
		( )	Door handle overrides rear door lock.		
		( )	No means for unlocking rear door from inside the vehicle.		
		207 ● SEATING SYSTEMS			
		( )	No seatback locks in both front seats.		
		208 - OCCUPANT CRASH PROTECTION			
		( )	____ front belts missing / nonconforming.		
		( )	____ rear belts missing / nonconforming.		
		( )	No U.S.-type seat belt warning system.		
		209 - SEAT BELT ASSEMBLIES			
		( )	Required markings not on seat belts.		

___ Form HS-189 not signed.

___ Form HS-189 signed by an unidentified person.

___ Entry made in the name of a company, but signature not authenticated by coporate seal or notarized statement identifying the officer of the company legally able to sign the statement of compliance for the company.

___ Notarized power-of-attorney from the importer, delegating signature authority, not submitted.

___ Backup data insufficient to establish conformance, as indicated above (T= text, P= photographs).

___ Text pages and/or photographs do not show vehicle identification no. (VIN)

___ Text & photographs not cross-referenced.

The following is a sample letter of transmittal to accompany the conformation package to the DOT.

October 5, 1983

U.S. Department of Transportation
National Highway Traffic Safety
Administration (Nef-32 CUS)
400 7th. St. S.W.
Washington, D.C. 20460

ATTN: *Lynn L. Bradford,* Associate Administrator for Enforcement

Subject: Entry #300798 6/17/83 (1976 Porsche 3.0 Carrera)
    VIN# 9116610202
    PCI# 8306-348-1

Please find enclosed the materials and forms relating compliance/conformity:

1. Form OMB #2127-0012 (8 pages)
2. Substantiating statements
3. Photos and documentation
4. Attachments
5. German manual
6. American (U.S.) manual

If you have any questions please feel free to contact me.

A. L. Smith, Jr.

Enclosures:

CC: Att: W.B. Lim
      Director, Classification & Value
      Department of the Treasury
      U.S. Customs Service
      P.O. Box 2450
      San Francisco, Calif. 94126

The following is a sample letter you may find
helpful if you require an extension from the DOT.

Sept. 12, 1983

U.S. Department of Transportation
NHTS Administration (NEF-32 CUS)
Washington, D.C. 20460

Attention: Lynn L. Bradford

This is a request for an extension to enable me to complete conformation of my recently imported
auto to US DOT specs. Your approval will be most appreciated.

VIN: 9116610202   Customs entry: 83-300798-2   Date of entry: 6/17/83

Thank you for your consideration.

Larry Smith

cc: Dept. of Treas.
      U.S. Customs Service
      P.O. Box 2450
      San Francisco, Calif. 94126
      Atten: Tom Welty
              Team 16

Chapter 7

Paperwork

Once you have chosen the car, then the necessary paperwork needs to be done to purchase and export the car. In Germany a special set of papers, in addition to the standard sales agreement or invoice (which show the agreed upon price, date and article sold) needs to be prepared. Samples of actual paperwork are shown here so you'll know what to expect. Be sure to keep copies of all forms you prepare.

Be prepared to furnish some or all of these documents when registering the car in the United States. It might be a good idea to find out from your local Department of Motor Vehicles what is required or will be accepted in order for the car to be fully registered. This way, you will know exactly what documents are needed from the seller. The documents shown here have proven to be entirely adequate and acceptable.

Paying for the car

There are several ways to purchase your car, depending upon which approach you chose to locate your car.

The best approach, if you go over to locate your own car, is to take cash or arrange to transfer the amount you will need to a bank in the country where you intend to purchase the car. Your own US bank may have a correspondent bank in the country, which should make arranging for transfer and access much easier. Most sellers will want to complete the transaction on the spot—at least within the week, and in cash.

If you do not travel to Europe but have someone else handle the transaction for you, then you should be prepared to put about $3,000 to $5,000 down if the car is used; twenty-five percent of the purchase price if the car is new. This amount could be sent via your bank to your friend or other person handling the transaction. The down payment is generally advisable because this will commit the seller (and the buyer) to sell the car only to you or your agent. Most cars in superior condition will be sold the same day they are advertised, so speed in these procedures is often essential. Within a week of making the down payment, you should have the balance of the funds sent over to complete the transaction.

A Letter of Credit (LC) is a means whereby cash doesn't have to be sent or taken, and works best in the case of a correspondent bank. No matter which method is utilized (except taking cash) you should plan on some fees and charges by the intermediaries. Go to your US bank and request one. If you have the funds they will draw one up. Direct payment using bank money orders or international bank drafts are also an approach that can be used. A bank draft or escrow account can also be used.

Some banks in the United States will gladly finance a car, even a used car. The trick is to get the car into the United States—the bank won't finance a car it can't see (even photos won't help) unless you're on very friendly terms with your banker. In some cases, interim loans have been made with collateral based on something other than the car. Then, when the car arrives and the bank can actually see the car (and the fact that it is probably worth more than you paid for it) the loan is switched to a car loan.

Final papers

To finish this process you will receive the following documents:

1. Form letter from US Department of Transportation to District Director of Customs authorizing customs to release the bond. Note that the importer is listed for copy.
2. Courtesy notice, Customs Form 433A (052881), is a notice of those entries scheduled to liquidate; that is, to be recorded for offical entry to the United States. This notice lists pertinent data with which you should be very familiar by the time you receive this notice.
3. Notice of Waiver. This notice should be received from EPA if you have imported the car under the one-time exemption.

SALES CONTRACT

The following sales contract is between:

the seller: Mr

and the buyer:
        Mr A.L. Smith Jr

        USA

The buyer is represented by:
        Mr William R McCreight

        BRD

Mr McCreight hereby accepts on Mr Smith's behalf the Porsche 911 3.0 Liter Carrera, 1976, chassis number 9116610202. The sales price is DM 23000.-- (twentythreethousand DM), paid in cash at the time the car was delivered.

The Seller,   On behalf of the buyer,

_______________________   _______________________
                                              William R McCreight

Frankfurt am Main, 13 June 1983

FOREIGN TRANSFER

FORMERLY UNITED CALIFORNIA BANK

FT No. **91977**

OFFICE Los Altos, #630	**DATE** March 22, 1983

U.S. OR FOREIGN AMOUNT IN WORDS
Twenty-eight thousand-two hundred-thirty-five and 29/100
German Marks

U.S. OR FOREIGN AMOUNT IN FIGURES
28,235.29 German Marks

RATE 0.4250

PAYABLE TO:
W. R. Mc Creight
Acct. #7798799-00
Dresner Bank
Bank's Number BLZ 50080000

BY ORDER OF:
A. L. Smith

REMARKS
Bank Address:
Hauptstrasse 69
D-6238 Hofheim Am Taunus,
West Germany

REMIT BY:
☐ AIR MAIL   ☒ CABLE

COPY

NOT NEGOTIABLE

U.S. DOLLAR AMOUNT	$12,000.00
CABLE CHARGES	$ 6.50
AIR MAIL CHARGES	$
SUBTOTAL	$12,006.50
COMMISSION	$ 10.00
TOTAL	$12,016.50

AUTHORIZED SIGNATURE

THIS TRANSACTION IS TO BE HANDLED SUBJECT TO THE FOLLOWING CONDITIONS:

1. This receipt is part of and is subject to all the provisions of this contract and said receipt is not negotiable.

2. Payment will be made subject to the rules and regulations of any governmental agencies, and banks or any other private agencies used in effecting the payment, and the bank shall not be liable for any act or omission of any agency or correspondent employed to make such payment or for any loss or damage resulting therefrom or from errors or delays on the part of telegraph, cable or radio companies in the transmission of any message relating to such payment, nor for any delay in delivery or failure to deliver any such message or for any acts or loss or damage resulting from any laws, decrees, orders or regulations purporting to be effective where payment is to be made, or from any civil, military or war conditions, or from any cause beyond the control of the bank.

3. The bank shall be under no obligation to obtain the receipt of the payee. The bank, on request, will use its best efforts to trace payment; no request for tracing shall be made prior to three months from date of the order on cable remittances nor prior to six months on other remittances.

4. If for any reason the credit covered by the foreign remittance herein is returned or recredited to the bank, the remitter agrees to accept refund in the amount of the equivalence in United States Dollars of the amount of the foreign money credit based on the current buying rate in New York on the date of the refund less any charges and expenses of the bank.

IB-307 2-82   **CUSTOMER'S RECEIPT**   5

IRREVOCABLE LETTER OF CREDIT NO.________

DATE: _______________________________________

Gentlemen:

We hereby irrevocably authorize you or your assigns to draw on_________________
____ at the request of
____ up to an aggregate amount of
____ U.S. Dollars ($______________)
available by your drafts at sight drawn by you or your assigns accompanied by the
written certification of you or your assigns stating that you have incurred liability,
loss, cost, expense or unpaid premiums as a result of execution of bonds or undertakings on behalf of ____
in favor of U.S. Customs Service.

Such statement must enumerate the amounts payable by you or your assigns for the account
of the above named Principal. All drafts so drawn must be marked under our credit-
number.

It is a condition of this Letter of Credit that it shall be deemed automatically·
extended, without amendment, for one (1) year from the present or any future
expiration date hereof, unless thirty (30) days prior to any such date we shall notify
you and your assigns in writing via registered mail that we elect not to consider this
Letter of Credit renewed for any such additional period. Upon receipt by you or your
assigns of such notice you or your assigns may draw hereunder, within the then
applicable expiration date and for the then available amount, without having incurred
liability by reason of having executed your bonds or undertakings, by means of drafts
drawn by you or your assigns on us at sight accompanied by written certification by
you or your assigns that the aforesaid bonds or undertakings are still outstanding,
that the proceeds of the draft will be retained and applied by you or your assigns
only in discharge or reimbursement of liability, loss, cost, expense or unpaid
premiums as a result of your execution of such bonds or undertakings, and that in the
event your liability under your bonds or undertakings is satisfied you or your assigns
will refund to us the amount paid, less any amounts which may have been paid by you
in the meantime under your bonds or undertakings and any unpaid premiums due you on
said bonds or undertakings.

We engage with you or your assigns that all drafts drawn under and in compliance with
the terms of this credit will be duly honored on delivery of documents as specified
if presented at this office on or before____________________________, or any
automatically extended date as herein set forth. We hereby engage with you or your
assigns that all drafts drawn and presented as above specified will be duly honored
by us.

Except so far as otherwise expressly stated, this credit is subject to the uniform
customs and practices for commercial documentary credits as set forth in I.C.C.
Publication No. 290.

Yours truly,

Authorized Signature   **Authorized Signature**

________________________   ________________________

Bank Title________________   **Bank Title**________________

SAMPLE GERMAN OWNERSHIP PAPERS

Fahrzeugbrief

Das Fahrzeug ist heute mit dem amtlichen Kennzeichen ______ zum Verkehr zugelassen worden für

Vorname, Name (ggf. auch Geburtsname), Firma

geb. am

Wohnort/Firmensitz am Tag der Zulassung

Postleitzahl und Ort, Datum

Stempel

Zulassungsstelle

Unterschrift

Das Fahrzeug ist heute mit dem amtlichen Kennzeichen ______ umgeschrieben worden auf:

Vorname, Name (ggf. auch Geburtsname), Firma

geb. am

Wohnort/Firmensitz am Tag der Umschreibung

Postleitzahl und Ort, Datum

Stempel

Zulassungsstelle

Unterschrift

Das Fahrzeug ist heute mit dem amtlichen Kennzeichen ______ umgeschrieben worden auf:

Vorname, Name (ggf. auch Geburtsname), Firma

geb. am

Wohnort/Firmensitz am Tag der Umschreibung

Postleitzahl und Ort, Datum

Stempel

Zulassungsstelle

Unterschrift

Das Fahrzeug ist heute mit dem amtlichen Kennzeichen ______ umgeschrieben worden auf:

Vorname, Name (ggf. auch Geburtsname), Firma

geb. am

Wohnort/Firmensitz am Tag der Umschreibung

Postleitzahl und Ort, Datum

Stempel

Zulassungsstelle

Unterschrift

Weitere Halter-Eintragungen

Das Fahrzeug ist heute mit dem amtlichen Kennzeichen   HG - JU 15   umgeschrieben worden auf

Vorname, Name (ggf. auch Geburtsname), Firma   ... geb. Link

... Bad Homburg v.d.H.   geb. am   29.06.53

Wohnort/Firmensitz am Tag der Umschreibung

Postleitzahl und Ort, Datum   31. JAN. 1983

Bad Homburg

Der Landrat des Hochtauniskreises
Im Auftrag

Zulassungsstelle   Unterschrift

Das Fahrzeug ist heute mit dem amtlichen Kennzeichen   umgeschrieben worden auf

Vorname, Name (ggf. auch Geburtsname), Firma

geb. am

Wohnort/Firmensitz am Tag der Umschreibung

Postleitzahl und Ort, Datum

Stempel

Zulassungsstelle   Unterschrift

Raum für die Eintragung von Stillegungen (§ 27 Abs. 6 StVZO)

Bei Vermerk der vorübergehenden Stillegung im Brief gilt das Fahrzeug als endgültig aus dem Verkehr gezogen, wenn es vor Ablauf eines Jahres nicht wieder in Betrieb genommen wird. Soll das Fahrzeug danach wieder in den Verkehr gebracht werden, ist nach § 27 Abs. 7 StVZO der unbrauchbar gewordene Brief zur Einziehung vorzulegen und ein neuer Brief unter Beibringung eines amtlich anerkannten Gutachtens eines amtlich anerkannten Sachverständigen auszustellen.

Stillegung	Wiederinbetriebnahme	Stillegung	Wiederinbetriebnahme
am	am	am	am 7 April 1981
Stempel	Stempel	Stempel	Stempel
Unterschrift	Unterschrift	Unterschrift	Unterschrift
am	am	am	am 7 Feb 1982
Stempel	Stempel	Stempel	Stempel
Unterschrift	Unterschrift	Unterschrift	Unterschrift
am	am	am 0. JUNI 1983	am
Stempel	Stempel	Stempel	Stempel
Unterschrift	Unterschrift	Unterschrift	Unterschrift

Nr. 54 753 428

Raum für sonstige Eintragungen
der Zulassungsstelle

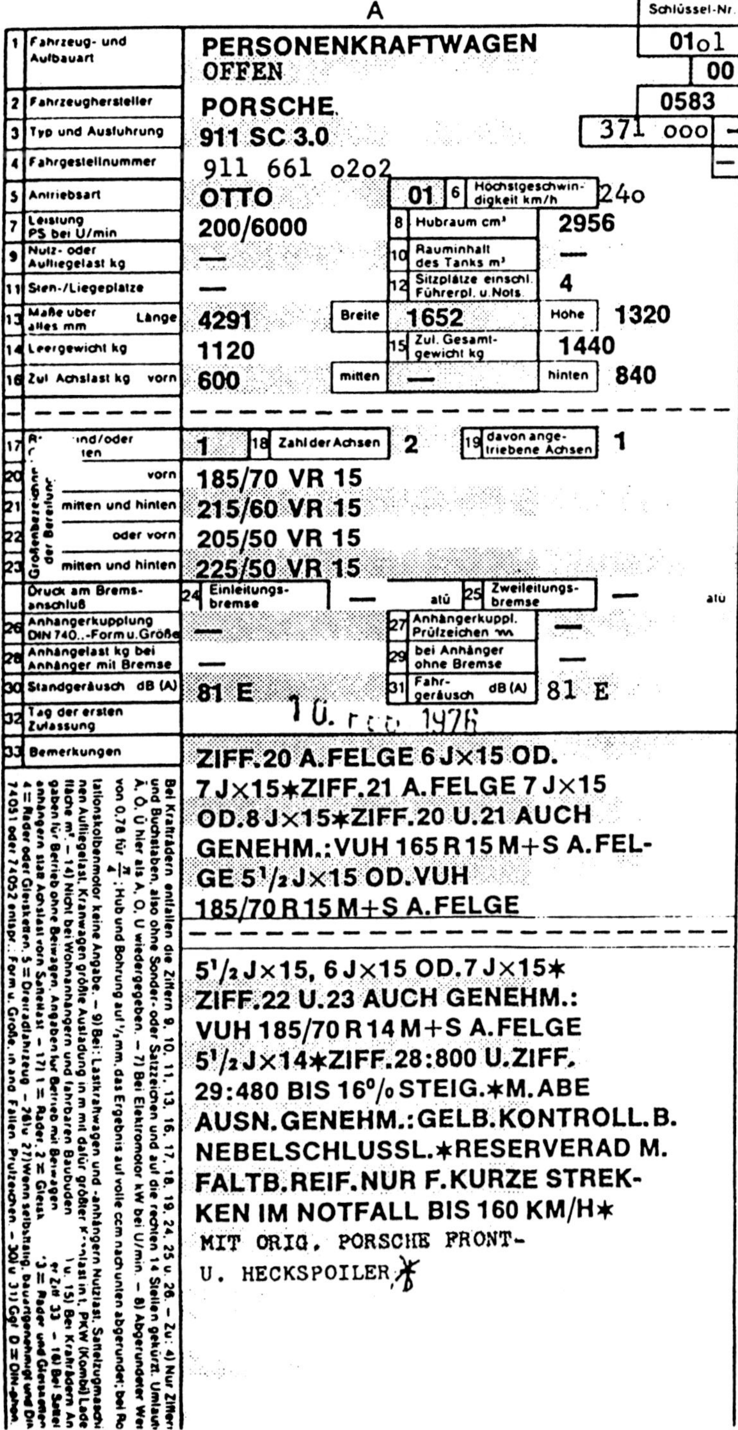

	A	Schlüssel-Nr.
1 Fahrzeug- und Aufbauart	**PERSONENKRAFTWAGEN OFFEN**	01o1 / 00
2 Fahrzeughersteller	**PORSCHE**	0583
3 Typ und Ausführung	**911 SC 3.0**	371 000 –
4 Fahrgestellnummer	911 661 o2o2	–
5 Antriebsart	**OTTO** 01	6 Höchstgeschwindigkeit km/h **24o**
7 Leistung PS bei U/min	**200/6000**	8 Hubraum cm³ **2956**
9 Nutz- oder Aufliegelast kg	—	10 Rauminhalt des Tanks m³ —
11 Steh-/Liegeplätze	—	12 Sitzplätze einschl. Führerpl. u. Nots. **4**
13 Maße über alles mm Länge **4291**	Breite **1652**	Höhe **1320**
14 Leergewicht kg **1120**	15 Zul. Gesamtgewicht kg **1440**	
16 Zul. Achslast kg vorn **600**	mitten —	hinten **840**
17 Rad und/oder ...	1	18 Zahl der Achsen **2**	19 davon angetriebene Achsen **1**
20 vorn	**185/70 VR 15**	
21 mitten und hinten	**215/60 VR 15**	
22 oder vorn	**205/50 VR 15**	
23 mitten und hinten	**225/50 VR 15**	
Druck am Bremsanschluß	24 Einleitungsbremse — atü	25 Zweileitungsbremse — atü
26 Anhängerkupplung DIN 740...-Form u. Größe	—	27 Anhängerkuppl. Prüfzeichen —
28 Anhängelast kg bei Anhänger mit Bremse	—	29 bei Anhänger ohne Bremse —
30 Standgeräusch dB (A)	**81 E**	31 Fahrgeräusch dB (A) **81 E**
32 Tag der ersten Zulassung	1 0. Feb. 1976	

33 Bemerkungen

**ZIFF.20 A.FELGE 6 J×15 OD.
7 J×15✶ZIFF.21 A.FELGE 7 J×15
OD.8 J×15✶ZIFF.20 U.21 AUCH
GENEHM.:VUH 165 R 15 M+S A.FEL-
GE 5½ J×15 OD.VUH
185/70 R 15 M+S A.FELGE**

**5½ J×15, 6 J×15 OD.7 J×15✶
ZIFF.22 U.23 AUCH GENEHM.:
VUH 185/70 R 14 M+S A.FELGE
5½ J×14✶ZIFF.28:800 U.ZIFF.
29:480 BIS 16⁰/o STEIG.✶M.ABE
AUSN.GENEHM.:GELB.KONTROLL.B.
NEBELSCHLUSSL.✶RESERVERAD M.
FALTB.REIF.NUR F.KURZE STREK-
KEN IM NOTFALL BIS 160 KM/H✶**
MIT ORIG. PORSCHE FRONT-
U. HECKSPOILER.✶

Fahrzeugbrief

Nr. 94 759 426

B   C

|1| |1|

Die Angaben über Hersteller, Typ und Ausführung des Fahrzeugs sowie die Fahrgestellnummer dürfen im Fahrzeugbrief grundsätzlich nicht geändert werden. Wenn die Fahrgestellnummer nicht mit der am Fahrzeug angebrachten übereinstimmt, gehört der Brief nicht zum Fahrzeug.

|5| |6|
|7| |8|
|9| |10|
|11| |12|
|13|
|14| |15|
|16|

|17| |18| |19|
|20|
|21|
|22|
|23|
|24| |25|
|26| |27|
|28| |29|
|30| |31|
|32|

|33| Bemerkungen

Die Richtigkeit der Angaben in Spalte B wird bescheinigt. Das Fahrzeug entspricht – insoweit*) – den geltenden Vorschriften.

________________ , den ________________

Stempel

____
Unterschrift

Die Richtigkeit der Angaben in Spalte C wird bescheinigt. Das Fahrzeug entspricht – insoweit*) – den geltenden Vorschriften.

________________ , den ________________

Stempel

____
Unterschrift

Nr. 04 759 420

34) Zusätzliche Bemerkungen zur Fahrzeugbeschreibung auf Seite 2

Bescheinigung des Inhabers einer Allgemeinen Betriebserlaubnis/EWG-Betriebserlaubnis.
Die Richtigkeit der Angaben in Spalte A (einschließlich der Bemerkungen unter Ziffern 33 und 34) über die Beschaffenheit des Fahrzeugs und über dessen Übereinstimmung mit dem Typ

911 SC 3.0 , Ausf.

für den die Allgemeine Betriebserlaubnis unter Nr. **9104**
MIT DEM NACHTRAG I-II /EWG-Betriebserlaubnis unter
Nr.*)
mit dem Betriebserlaubnisbogen Nr.*)
und dem Beschreibungsbogen Nr.*)
am **1. 3. 1974** in **FLENSBURG**
durch **DAS KRAFTFAHRT-BUNDESAMT**
erteilt worden ist, wird heute bescheinigt.

7000 STUTTGART 40 , den Feb. 1976

Firma
Dr. Ing. h. c. F. Porsche
Aktiengesellschaft

*) Zutreffendes ausfüllen.   Unterschrift

Bescheinigung des amtlich anerkannten Sachverständigen für den Kraftfahrzeugverkehr (a. a. S.).
Es wird bescheinigt, daß – nach dem vorliegenden Gutachten des a. a. S.

                     001/404256   vom
10.2.76 ───── (Name)
(Datum u. ggf. Nr. des Gutachtens)   *) – die Angaben in Spalte A – unter Ziffern *) –
                     33.
                                                    zutreffen
und das Fahrzeug – mit Ausnahme der unter Ziffer 33 beschriebenen
Abweichungen.*) – den geltenden Vorschriften entspricht.

Stempel   Stuttgart   , den 10.2.76

*) ggf. streichen   Unterschrift des amtl. anerk. Sachverständigen

---

Vermerke des Herstellers

115 001 006 / 116 2032 grandprix weiss

Raum für weitere amtlich zugelassene Eintragungen

Durch das Auffinden des Original-
fahrzeugbriefes wurde der Ersatz-
fahrzeugbrief Nr.: 79761125 einge-
zogen und am 30.05.83 vernichtet.

6380 Bad Homburg, 30.5.83

Der Landrat   30. MAI 1983
Des Hochtauuskreises
Im Auftrage:

US Department
of Transportation

National Highway
Traffic Safety
Administration

400 Seventh St. S.W.
Washington, DC 20590

1 December 1983
In Reply Refer To:
NEF-32-CUS
FCI No: 8306-348-1

District Director of Customs
Attn: Motor Vehicle Imp Specl
P.O. Box 2450
San Francisco, CA 94126

Dear Sir:

The National Highway Traffic Safety Administration (NHTSA) acknowledges receipt of a statement of compliance submitted by the importer for the below identified vehicle imported on Customs entry shown:

    Importer's Name: A. L. SMITH JR.
    Customs Entry No. & Date: 300798, 6/17/1983
    Port Code: SFR-2801
    Vehicle Make & Model: PORSCHE 911SC
    Vehicle Identification No. (VIN): 911661 0202

The statement meets the requirements of 19 CFR 12.80(e). Release from all liability under the bond posted with respect to compliance with the requirements of NHTSA is, therefore, satisfactory. Release must be obtained from the Environmental Protection Agency (EPA) relative to compliance with the emission control requirements (19 CFR 12.73), if applicable.

It should be noted that this bond release letter does not constitute agreement by NHTSA that the vehicle, in fact, is in conformance with all applicable Federal Motor Vehicle Safety Standards (FMVSS) since actual conformance is determinable only by compliance testing.

By copy of this letter the importer is advised that NHTSA reserves the right to make an actual compliance inspection of the vehicle at a future date to verify the accuracy of data contained in his statement of compliance.

                    Sincerely,

                    Francis Armstrong
                    Director
                    Office of Vehicle Safety Compliance
                    Enforcement

CC: A. L. SMITH JR.

REFER INQUIRIES TO:	COURTESY NOTICE			ENTRIES SCHEDULED TO LIQUIDATE	

REFER INQUIRIES TO:

U. S. CUSTOMS SERVICE
555 BATTERY ST
SAN FRANCISCO
CALIFORNIA   94126

GOODS ENTERED AT:

72601
S F AIRPORT

ARTHUR LAURENCE SMITH   L

SERIES	TYPE AND ENTRY NO.	DATE OF ENTRY	LIQUID CODE	INITIAL AMOUNT	LIQUIDATION AMOUNT
	>>> NOT	THIS IS	NOT	A BILL <<<	
83	1 00300799	06-17-83		250.00	260.00

IMPORTER NUMBER	DATE OF LIQUIDATION
01-34-340	01-01-94

Your entry is scheduled to liquidate on the date indicated for the liquidation amount. Any difference between this amount and the initial amount paid will be billed or refunded to you.
If you are dissatisfied with the liquidated amount, a protest may be filed within 90 days of the date of liquidation according to

+ INDICATES REFUND TO DIFFERENT ADDRESS

• INDICATES OFFSET OF REFUNDS

7

DEPARTMENT OF THE TREASURY
U.S. CUSTOMS SERVICE
CUSTOMS FORM 4333A (05 288

JAN 2 4 1984

OFFICE OF
AIR, NOISE AND RADIATION

Mr. Paul Andres
U S Customs Service
555 Battery St
P.O Box 24560
San Francisco, Calif 94126

Approval is hereby given for release of the EPA obligation on the following <u>1978 or older model year</u> bonded vehicle.

Importer: *Larry Smith*
Make: *Porsche*
Model: *911 Carrera*
Year: *1976*

VIN: *9116610202*
Entry#: *83-300798-2*
Entry Date: *June 17, 83*

While we lack sufficient information to determine whether this vehicle has been brought into conformity with Federal emission requirements, because of the age of the vehicle at the time of importation we recommend release of the Environmental Protection Agency obligation on the bond. Please note that this does not release the importer of the obligation to comply with Federal safety requirements administered by the Department of Transportation.

We appreciate your cooperation in the enforcement of the joint Customs-EPA regulations.

Very truly yours,

for Gerard C. Kraus, Chief
Investigation/Imports Section
Manufacturers Operations Division
(EN-340F)

cc: Importer *Mr. Larry Smith*

<u>Note to Importer</u>: Because of the age of your vehicle at the time of importation, we are releasing you of the obligation to bring your vehicle into conformity with Federal emission requirements. However, you still must comply with Federal safety requirements and any applicable state or local emission-related requirements. We have been informed by the California Air Resources Board (CARB) that a used vehicle* (one having accumulated more than 7500 miles) which has not been brought into conformity with Federal or California emission requirements cannot be registered in California. A new vehicle* (one having accumulated less than 7500 miles) must have been certified with CARB by the manufacturer in order to be registered in California. Further, this determination applies only to a first-time importation of a nonconforming vehicle by an individual for personal use. It would not apply to any subsequent vehicle imported by you or to any importation for resale. This is an important document. Please keep a copy of it with your vehicle registration at all times.

* As defined in Section 43156 of the California Health and Safety Code.

Cost estimator

The following chart has been designed to make it easy to determine in advance the cost of the auto you desire to import. Some charges listed may not, of course, be applicable in every case.

Item	Foreign Currency	US Dollars
Base price	_______	_______
De-licensing in Europe (returning the plates to the local authorities)	_______	_______
Export license for travel in Europe before shipment to US	_______	_______
Shipping costs (including insurance and trans-shipment) by air (obtain quote from airline)	_______	_______
by ship (obtain quote from shipper)	_______	_______
Accessories added before shipment to US	_______	_______

Item	Foreign Currency	US Dollars
Import duty after arrival in US (2.5% for 1986)	_______	_______
Miscellaneous dockage, port fees		_______
Location, selection and consulting fees	_______	_______
Bond for US Customs		_______
Services of customshouse broker		_______
State sales tax		_______
State registration fee		_______
Conformation to DOT specifications		_______
EPA certification (not required if brought in under one-time exemption)		_______
Meeting state pollution requirements		_______

Manufacturers

The following are contacts of various manufacturers who are available to assist in importation and conformation of DOT and EPA requirements. Write and/or call if you need assistance.

CALIFORNIA
Kurt Meier, Liaison Engineer
US Compliance Office
11300 Playa St.
Culver City, CA 90230
(213) 390-3048
   Porsche

Brian Gill, Manager
Certification Department
American Honda Motor Co., Inc.
100 W. Alondra Blvd.
Gardena, CA 90247
(213) 321-8680
   Honda

Dave Illingworth, Manager
Customer Relations Dept.
2055 W. 190th St.
Torrance, CA 90504
(213) 532-5010
   Toyota

CONNECTICUT
Steven Rossi
Certification Engineer
Saab-Scania of America, Inc.
P.O. Box 697
Orange, CT 06477
(203) 795-5671
   Saab

MICHIGAN
L. Lawrence Nutson,
   Administrator
Emission and Development Sec.
Volkswagen of America, Inc.
P.O. Box 7050
293 E. Liberty Plaza
Ann Arbor, MI 48107
(313) 665-7515
   Volkswagen

Alberto Negro, Director
Fiat Research and Development
1 Parklane Bldg.
Dearborn, MI 48126
(313) 336-2400
   Fiat, Ferrari, Lancia

Joseph O'Hagen
Automotive Emissions and Fuel
  Economy Office
Engineering Staff
Ford Motor Co.
The American Rd.
Dearborn, MI 48121
(313) 322-5180
  Capri, Cortina, Ford Canada

Gene Byrd
Emissions Investigations and
  Liaison
Chrysler Corp.
P.O. Box 1118   Challenger
Detroit, MI 48231
(313) 956-6155
  Arrow, Champ, Sapporo

Larry A. Schaefer
Certification Program Manager
Renault USA, Inc.
14250 Plymouth Rd.
Detroit, MI 48232
(313) 493-2314
  Renault, AMC, AMC Canada

Masatoshi Ogate
Branch Manager
Toyo Kogyo USA
23777 Greenfield Rd. Suite 462
Southfield, MI 48075
(313) 559-5040
  Mazda

Robert Cowell
Automotive Emission Control
Environmental Activities Staff
General Motors Technical Center
Warren, MI 48090
(313) 575-1261
  Opel, Vauxhall, GM Canada

NEVADA
Kurt Meier
Porsche of America
Compliance Department
200 So. Virginia St.
Reno, NV 89501
(702) 348-3119
  Porsche

NEW JERSEY
Jean Stang
Customer Service Department
Donald Black, Technical Director
Alfa Romeo, Inc.
250 Sylvan Ave.
Englewood Cliffs, NJ 07632
(201) 871-1234
  Alfa Romeo

Dianne Black, Manager
Emission and Certification
Jaguar Rover Triumph, Inc.
600 Willow Tree Rd.
Leonia, NJ 07605
(201) 461-7300
  Austin Morris, Jaguar, Rover,
  Triumph, MG

Kenneth W. Preece
Regulations and Special Project
  Manager
Rolls-Royce Motors, Inc.
P.O. Box 476
Lyndhurst, NJ 07071
(201) 460-9600
  Rolls-Royce

Michael Grossman
Government and Engineering
  Liaison
US Technical Research Co.
33 Garland Way
Lyndhurst, NJ 07071
(201) 438-1113
  Peugeot, Citroen

Karl-Heinz Ziwica
Director of Engineering
BMW of North America, Inc.
Montvale, NJ 07645
(201) 573-2000 or 573-2072
  BMW

Army Johnson
Lotus Performance Cars
530 Walnut St.
Norwood, NJ 07648
(201) 784-0726
  Lotus

Product Compliance Dept.
Mercedes-Benz of North Amer-
  ica, Inc.
  One Mercedes Dr.
Montvale, NJ 07645
(201) 573-2784
  Mercedes-Benz

Paul Utans
Vice President for Government
  Affairs
Subaru of America, Inc.
Pennsauken, NJ 08109
(609) 665-3344
  Subaru

Norm Friberg
Product Compliance Manager
Volvo of America Corp.
Volvo Dr.
Rockleigh, NJ 07647
(201) 768-7300
  Volvo

NEW YORK
Robert Clerk
Aston Martin Lagonda, Inc.
14 Weyman Ave.
New Rochelle, NY 10805
(914) 576-3202
  Aston Martin

WASHINGTON, DC
Takauchi
Staff, Engine and Emission
  Control
Nissan Motor Co., Ltd.
Suite 707
1919 Pennsylvania Ave. NW
Washington, DC 20037
(202) 466-5284
  Nissan, Datsun

Testing laboratories

The following test laboratories have demonstrated capability of conducting motor vehicle emission tests in accordance with federal test procedures. Tests performed at other laboratories are not acceptable without prior written approval from EPA. State emission checks or tests performed at service stations or repair shops are not acceptable.

Automotive Compliance Center, Inc.
4028 NE 6th Ave.
Fort Lauderdale, FL 33334
(305) 564-8993

Automotive Compliance Laboratory, Inc.
217 Smith Rd. (Ramapo Airport)
Spring Valley, NY 10977
(914) 425-3622

Automotive Environmental Systems, Inc.
7300 Bolsa Ave.
Westminster, CA 92683
(714) 897-0333

Automotive Research, Inc.
1331 Upland, #E
Houston, TX 77043
(713) 984-1502

Automotive Testing Labs, Inc.
P.O. Box 289
East Liberty, OH 43319
(513) 666-4351

Bay Area Emissions Laboratory, Inc.
26596 Corporate Ave.
Hayward, CA 94544
(415) 783-4950

Bendix
Advanced Products Div.
900 W. Maple Rd.
P.O. Box 2602
Troy, MI 43084
(313) 362-1800

Custom Engineering
Performance and Emissions Laboratories
7091-A Belgrave Ave.
Garden Grove, CA 92641
(714) 891-5704

EG&G Automotive Research,
  Inc.*
5404 Bandera Rd.
San Antonio, TX 78238
(512) 684-2310

Ethyl Corporation
1600 W. Eight Mile Rd.
Ferndale, MI
(313) 399-9600

Fairway Environmental
  Engineering
3032 Kashiwa St.
Torrance, CA 90505
(213) 775-7618

New York City Dept. of
  Environmental Protection
Mobile Source Controls Div.
75 Frost St.
Brooklyn, NY 11211
(212) 388-4994

Olson Engineering, Inc.
15442 Chemical Ln.
Huntington Beach, CA 92649
(714) 891-4821

Satra Automotive Emissions Lab.,
  Inc.
US 1 and 9 S.
Newark, NJ 07114
(201) 242-7908

Scott Environmental Technology,
  Inc.
Plumsteadville, PA 18949
(215) 766-8861

Southwest Research Institute*
6220 Culebra Rd.
San Antonio, TX
(512) 684-5111 x2653

Vehicle Emissions & Fuel
  Economy Lab.
Texas Transportation Institute
Texas A and M University
College Station, TX 77843
(713) 845-6176

*Also capable of testing
  motorcycles

Auto Importers Compliance Association (AICA)

AICA is an organization devoted to implementing proper standards for shops in the United States that attempt to conform autos imported from overseas. Much of the so-called "gray market" activity has come about because such shops were not rigidly controlled. Many shops sprang up overnight and some weren't prepared to do the right job and expected to "rip off" the customer.

The AICA was formed to organize the situation, and to provide an effective lobbying force in Congress for the members. Many auto manufacturers from Europe were in favor of outlawing all importation of cars except through a recognized factory dealer.

If you do not intend to handle any of the work yourself, it is suggested you contact an AICA member and make sure you follow the guidelines given in this book regarding the questions to determine if they are experienced—to allay your own concerns.

The following is a list of shops that specialize in doing the right work for either conforming to EPA specs, DOT specs or both and can be counted on to back up their work.

CALIFORNIA & WESTERN REGION

ACS Sales & Service, Orange, CA	714-998-8860
Automated Custom Systems, Inc., Orange, CA	714-974-5560
Avanti European Imports, Santa Clara, CA	408-727-0702
Bay City Auto Compliance Center, San Francisco, CA	415-431-8650
Classy Chassis, Santa Cruz, CA	408-476-5515
Coast Conversions & Sales, Santa Ana, CA	714-549-7704
Compliance Engineering, Inc., Irvine, CA	714-250-9533
Custom Conversions, Huntington Beach, CA	714-898-1565
D.C. Automotive Engineering, El Toro, CA	714-855-6681
DDK Motors, Newport Beach, CA	714-852-9132
Elite Imports & Conversions, Huntington Beach, CA	714-895-3762
Environmental Testing, Berkeley, CA	415-525-4916
Euro-Pacific Imports, Carlsbad, CA	619-729-7921
European Auto Conversions, Soquel, CA	408-476-4494
European Car Center, Santa Monica, CA	213-453-0316
FCI International Testing, Santa Ana, CA	714-754-6424
H&B BMW Specialists, Berkeley, CA	415-526-5489
ICL, Orange, CA	714-532-2053

Import Automotive Technology
Inc., Orange, CA 714-633-0818/9
K & R Auto Engineering,
Santa Ana, CA 714-660-8840
Mercedes Conversions,
Portland, OR 503-233-3747
Milano Imports, Gilroy, CA 408-847-8732
North American Imports
Compliance, Oakland, CA 415-430-0475
Silver Star Conversion Co.,
Santa Fe Springs, CA 213-945-2474
South Bay Conversion, Hermosa
Beach, CA 213-374-9720
South Coast Compliance,
Santa Ana, CA 714-662-3527
Tesla Lab, Fountain Valley, CA 714-895-1196
Victory Auto Service Center,
Van Nuys, CA 818-989-4141
West Coast Imports, Carlsbad, CA 619-931-1344

CENTRAL REGION

Automated Custom Systems, Inc.,
Elk Grove Village, IL 312-952-1790
European Auto Services,
Ferndale, MI 313-399-3130/1
German Motor Sales,
Cincinnati, OH 513-861-6000
Import Services, Fayetteville, AR 501-521-9877
J. Frank Motors, Indianapolis, IN 317-291-4108
Midwest Eurosport, Elk Grove, IL 312-981-0555
North Side Motors, Chicago, IL 312-728-2411
Tank Erectors, Waterville, KS 913-785-2207

FLORIDA REGION

Automated Custom Systems, Inc.,
Deerfield Beach, FL 305-481-2663
Automotive Compliance Center,
Ft. Lauderdale, FL 305-564-8993
Motorsport Engineering, Inc.,
Pompano Beach, Fl 305-971-2222
Transatlantic Motorcars,
Altamonte Spgs, FL 305-830-4500

NORTHEAST REGION

Conversion Technology,
North Wales, PA 215-699-9269
European Auto Specialties of
Toms River, NJ 201-240-3885
European Car Doctors,
Brighton, MA 617-254-0550
Federal Conversions U.S.A.,
Lester, PA 215-521-4646
Gary Steven's European Auto, Inc.,
Williston Park, NY 516-741-3740
German Auto Specialties, LTD,
Conshohocken, PA 215-828-2000
Henry's Foreign Auto Center,
Woodbridge, NJ 201-636-7017
I.A.T.L., Telford, PA 215-721-9112
International Import Cars,
North Hampton, NH 603-964-9477
Manhattan Motor Car Co.,
New York, NY 212-673-1560
Motor Werks, New Milford, CT 203-354-0240
Orion Motors, Sellersville, PA 215-257-5007
PAW, LTD, Glen Cove, NY 516-671-7300
Pierre Enterprises, Inc.,
Ronkonkoma, NY 516-588-8288
Soucy's Imports Inc.,
Manchester, NH 603-668-6909
Sport Auto, Inc., Blawnox, PA 412-826-1300
Village Imports of New England,
Portsmouth, RI 401-683-5120

SOUTHEAST REGION

Auto Conformity, Charleston, SC 803-554-8933
Autos European, Inc.,
Fayetteville, NC 919-864-2247
European Autocars, Inc.,
Rockville, MD 301-424-0600
European Auto Conversions,
Marietta, GA 404-425-0516
Exotic European Auto Imports,
Atlanta, GA 404-261-6673
Tysons Motors, Vienna, VA 703-827-0022

TEXAS REGION

ARI, Houston, TX 713-984-1502
Elite Auto Imports, Houston, TX 713-464-1545
Mario's Motors, Houston, TX 713-780-7934
Wallace Environmental Testing
Labs, Inc., Houston, TX 713-956-7705

Sources of information

New York Times, *1983, article*
Department of the Treasury, U.S. Custom Service publications
    Immediate Delivery and Consumption Entry Bond (Single entry) form 7551 (11-12-80)
    CF7501
    CF5101
    CF5106
    O.M.B. 48-R0255
    4333A (05 288)
    U.S. Customs Ports of Entry and Officers in Foreign Countries
U.S. Environmental Protection Agency publications
    Automotive Import Facts Sheet
    EPA 3520-1
    O.M.B. 2000-0228
    O.M.B. 2000-0041
    O.M.B. 04-R2403
    Manufacturer's U.S. Representatives
U.S. Department of Transportation
    General Guide for Substantiation of Compliance with FMVSS 214 and 215 and 49CFR581
    Summary Description of Standards
Miscellaneous
    Release Notice from EPA
    Release Notice from DOT
    California Air Resources Board, 1984 Smog Check information